A Race For Life:

From Cancer to the Ironman

A RACE FOR LIFE:

FROM CANCER TO THE IRONMAN

COPYRIGHT INFORMATION: *A Race For Life* was copyrighted June 1990 by Ruth Heidrich, M.S.

ISBN 0-9604190-1-2
LIBRARY OF CONGRESS CATALOG CARD NO. is pending.

All rights reserved. No part of this book may be reproduced in any form without permission in writing from the author.

>   *Heidrich Weisbrod Associates*
>   1415 Victoria St. #1106
>   Honolulu, HI 96822

Ruth Heidrich has also co-authored several books on weight control, cigarette smoking elimination, defense mechanisms, and self-hypnosis techniques. She is also a reporter for "Triathlon Today!"

It is recommended that before you start any diet and exercise program, you first check with a physician who can evaluate your safe level of exercise and any dietary considerations.

PRINTED IN HAWAII BY THE OFFSET HOUSE INC.

THIS BOOK IS DEDICATED TO
THE NEXT GENERATION OF
TRIATHLETES:

Jay Meindertsma, 14; Sean Hanratty, 14; Jennie McCurdy, 13; Joshua Meindertsma, 12; Mandy Jones, 12; Ryan Hanratty. 10; Tommy McCurdy, 9; Davis Chappins, 3; Randy Zamparelli, 9; Kacie Zamparelli, 5; Jessica Heidrich, 2; and an as-yet-unnamed Heidrich on the way!

May they forever avoid the scourge of heart disease, stroke, cancer, and the whole host of diseases preventable by following a healthy lifestyle.

FOREWORD

For several years now, both medical and physical evidence has pointed to diet, exercise and emotional factors as contributing in great measure to prevention, some rather miraculous remissions and, in some cases, outright cures for cancer.

Ruth Heidrich tells a fascinating story of her progression from a woman devastated by the thought of losing her breast and, quite possibly her life, from cancer to becoming an internationally recognized athlete.

Her exercise and diet programs are now so well integrated into her life that many of her friends do not know that she routinely competes in the Kona, Hawaii, "Ironman Triathlon" with a back-to-back 2.4 mile rough water ocean swim, 112 mile bike and a 26.2 mile marathon.

Ruth's story needs to be told, not to glorify her athletic prowess, which is a story in itself, but to demonstrate that there is a mix of diet, exercise, and mental conditioning that any one of us can use to fight the invasion of disease and depression in a natural way.

As the medical profession, coaches, and nutritionists gather evidence for our future benefit, people like Ruth Heidrich are on the forefront, proving that the way to a healthier and happier life, and the prevention of disease, are here today.

Terry Shintani, M.D.
Honolulu, Hawaii

ACKNOWLEDGEMENTS

Writing this book has turned out to be an incredible adventure. I could never have done it without the support of some wonderful people. John A. McDougall, M.D., was the physician who turned my life around by educating me about my cancer. He also followed my progress as a volunteer subject in his breast cancer research.

Dr. McDougall was the first to suggest that I write a book about what I learned on this medical journey, suggesting that it would be of value to others. He believed in me enough to literally take me by the hand to a computer store where he showed me the wonders of computers and word processing. He then started a phone campaign, calling me to check up on my progress, assuring me that "it's so easy, once you get started." Dr. McDougall was right. Writing this book was easy, but that's only from this vantage point. Looking at it from the beginning, it seemed nearly impossible.

As I increased my exercise, I ran into resistance from people who thought that I, as a cancer patient, should be "taking it easy." Since I'd read that cancer cells were anaerobic, I felt compelled to get as much oxygen through exercise as I could. As my "unorthodox" medical program gained more attention, I started to get some publicity. This led to a appearance on "The Hour Magazine" with host, Gary Collins. On that show I got to tell the "whole world" about Kenneth Cooper, M.D. and how he launched me on my exercise program. Dr. Cooper, with his landmark book on aerobic exercise, altered my life forever, too.

Next, John Kay came into my life. He'd read my story in the Hawaii publication, *MIDWEEK*. After he introduced himself to me, he asked if I'd ever considered writing a book. I told him that, by chance, I'd just started seriously considering it. He volunteered to help; and help he did. We met weekly for him to review the previous week's painful efforts. (Writing is easy; you just sit down at a typewriter and open a vein!) He critiqued my writing, patted me on the back, and sent me off to write some more.

Terry Shintani, M.D., entered the scene with the opportunity to be co-host on KGU Radio's, "Nutrition and You." Working with Dr. Shintani has been invaluable, as he gave me support both as a physician and a friend. We've had some fabulous guests on our show and I learned a lot. I really owe Bonnie Choy, R.N. for that one!

The next major assist came from Carl Weisbrod, Ph.D. Carl came into my life as a guest on our radio talk show to discuss one of my favorite topics, the behavioral aspects of following a healthy lifestyle. My manuscript was by then complete and looking for a publisher. He suggested that I self publish, and then helped me, drawing on his own publishing experiences.

There were many others. Mike Barnhart was the lifesaver who helped decode the machine and computer language confronting me in my software, hardware, and the woman-machine interface. The McMullens, Mike and Judy, provided psychological and technical support. The encouragement of my parents, friends, and even strangers was helpful and much appreciated. Naming all of them would be impossible, but I received a special assist from my best training buddy and favorite bicycle mechanic, Kate Laws and the support of the experts at Island Triathlon & Bike. The folks at Triathlon Today!, especially Lew Kidder and Steve Jonas, were also helpful.

With inspiration and support like that, there may be more. The journey is far from over!

TABLE OF CONTENTS

Chapter 1
A Race For Life..1
An overview of what's to come: An average person, who, when confronted with the diagnosis of cancer, responds by deciding to go for superfitness by training for the Ironman Triathlon.

Chapter 2
Goal Setting: Making Hard Seem Easy.................17
Initially the completion of an Ironman is overwhelming. You'll learn how to set goals. Involves setting sub-goals, programming the mind, and create even greater goals.

Chapter 3
How Do We Know What We Know?......................25
In the areas of health, fitness, nutrition, and athletic training, myths are rampant. In any locker room one hears so many "how to's," what not to do, etc. This chapter tells you how to sort out truth from myth.

Chapter 4
Athletic Supporters (And Non-Supporters).............31
Since most people in this society are sedentary, you will have to learn how to strengthen your desire to withstand temptation. How to find like-minded people who will support you in your quest for superfitness.

Chapter 5
The Diet:
Eating To Run Or Is It The Other Way Around?......36
How to lose weight and still eat as much as you want. Many consider this diet to be "radical," protein-deficient, inedible, dull, or a state of deprivation. Actually, it's the best way to supply the body with all essential nutrients, avoid harmful substances, save a whole lot of money and food preparation time. Using your appetite as a guide. How diet and exercise influence each other; why the average American is overfat.

Chapter 6
Body Fat%: Or What The Scales Don't Tell You......50
Most people are a little neurotic about their weight. What they don't realize is that the number on the scales is really meaningless. One can be at an "ideal" weight and be overfat, and conversely, over "ideal" weight and not be overfat. Learn how to tell the difference.

Chapter 7
Starting A Triathlon Training Program..................59
Assessing where you are, deciding how far you want to go, and how to get the two to meet. Can walking be part of a training program?

Chapter 8
Swimming: How To, Where To, Etc......................69
Two different approaches are required depending on whether you have a swimming background. Swimming is a sport requiring constant surveillance and fine-tuning. How being in a group helps.

Chapter 9
Bicycling: Getting Mechanical............................75
The only triathlon sport that puts you at risk for failing for a reason outside of yourself. Even with little or no mechanical aptitude, anyone can become minimally competent at bicycle repairs. Cycling also has such practical uses, e.g., commuting to work.

Chapter 10
Running: Getting Fast & Staying Uninjured...........81
*Yes, anyone can run, but not everyone can run **fast**. How a coach and a group can help. How it's possible to run at the end of a triathlon in spite of being exhausted.*

Chapter 11
Putting It All Together:
You're Doing A Triathlon!................................91
How the body copes with the demands that all three sports place on it. Transition training and its importance. The marketplace's response to this exciting new sport. Keeping a "cool head."

Chapter 12
Time Management: How To Get It All In............97
*For all those who say that exercise is okay IF you have no job and no family. Full-time athletes don't **need** to train full time; in fact, you're courting injury if you do.*

Chapter 13
Not For Men Only:
The Sexual Aspects of Fitness...........................103
How this diet and exercise program can keep men (and women) more youthful, sexier, and improve blood supply to critical parts. Breast cancer and osteoporosis are commonly thought to be limited to just women — they aren't. What alcohol can do to your sex life.

Chapter 14
Anemia & The Boston Marathon........................112
The human body has limitations; if you push it too far, it sends messages. Most marathoners have GI bleeding during races. How a frequently prescribed medication can cause anemia.

Chapter 15
Osteoporosis: The Hidden Handicap...................118
How the drug industry sells the public on the myth that calcium pills prevent osteoporosis; how exercise and low-protein diet are the cure and, just in case, how to get enough dietary calcium through healthy foods.

Chapter 16
Arthritis: Diet *Does* Make A Difference...............125
Another medical myth shattered! How a medical emergency got me off a physician-prescribed lifetime on an arthritis drug.

Chapter 17
The Crash I Can't Remember:
Safety Comes First...129
As if the other medical problems weren't enough, I was afforded the "opportunity" to experience both retrograde and anterograde (before and after) amnesia, and completely missed being rushed to the hospital in an ambulance.

Chapter 18
Plastic Surgery:
Reconstructing A Body And A Life....................138
A mastectomy can be horribly disfiguring; how rebuilding a body devastated by cancer surgery can have a strongly positive impact on a healthy body image; why women need no longer fear the traumatic effects of such surgery.

Chapter 19
Ironmen Can Be Beautiful:
Beauty Tips for Female Athletes.......................143
Just because you're a "jock-ette" doesn't mean you can't look gorgeous. How being superfit is the most effective beauty tip there is. Plus a number of other tips, just in case.

Chapter 20
Ironman: Kona, Hawaii...................................150
The "granddaddy" of all triathlons. Although I've done Kona four times, each one has been unique. How to cope with differing external and internal conditions.

Chapter 21
What's the Prognosis:
Why Cancer Isn't "Curable"............................160
Why some researchers are shifting their priorities to prevention and giving up on seeking a cure. Why some cancer patients live for three months and some for thirty years.

Appendix One
Interpretation of Lab Tests............................171

Appendix Two
Glossary..175

Bibliography... 178

A RACE FOR LIFE:

FROM CANCER TO THE IRONMAN

CHAPTER ONE

The words "**infiltrating ductile carcinoma**" burned a hole in my entire being. Wild and uncontrollable panic seized me. I could not believe what I just heard. "Oh, NO!" I cried, "Oh, no, no..." The haunting words of the diagnosis of cancer echoed repeatedly in my head as I fought back the dizziness and nausea.

Just minutes before, while waiting to hear the results of the biopsy from the pathology lab, I was so sure, in fact, certain, that the offending growth was benign. I kept telling myself everything was going to be just fine. Hadn't I done everything I was supposed to? There was no one to scream "NO FAIR!" to!

I'd always eaten a "well-balanced" diet and had sworn off "red meat" years before. I'd gotten "plenty" of exercise and, in fact, even run marathons. I had frequent medical check-ups that included mammograms and had religiously done my monthly breast self exams.

How could this have happened? Why me? Things like this only happen in movies — or to other people. I'd always led a somewhat uneventful life — healthy, successful, playing by all the rules. I'd even been dealt a good hand in the game of life, having frequently been told how attractive I was and that I had a nice body. I was well-educated, held an engrossing, well-paying job which involved traveling all over the world. I had two bright, beautiful and successful children.

So why this avalanche of devastation? It was both a life and death sentence for me. "Life" because there's still no real cure for breast cancer, and "death" because breast cancer is a major killer of adult women, striking one out of every nine or ten American women.

"My God, what do I do now?" I asked the two surgeons who were attending me.

"Surgery," the senior surgeon said. "I'd recommend a modified radical mastectomy since the tumor was so large."

I'd watched the surgeons carve a chunk as big as a golf ball out of my breast. Thinking that I must be exaggerating the size of it in my mind, I tried to diminish the image. No, it was still horribly big, no matter how I visualized it.

The type of surgery the doctors recommended would remove the breast that remained after the biopsy, the fascia covering the chest muscles, the skin covering the breast area, the nipple, and all the lymph nodes in the axilla, or armpit.

About this time I felt betrayed by my breasts anyway, so there was no problem in getting me to agree to the surgery...not even twice. When the surgeons suggested that at a later time they take the other breast, I was ready to hand them both over, although I was given no assurance that this would save my life.

The doctors (there were now three of them in the room) shook their heads and said, "We don't know if you have three months, three years, or how long. We don't know IF it has spread or how FAR if it has. We certainly don't know WHY; we just don't know..."

Adding to my anxiety was the fact that when I came in for this last check-up, the doctor, looking at the plainly visible lump in my breast, asked with great concern in his voice, "Why did you wait so long to come in?" I went into instant panic and at the same time flew into a rage.

"What do you mean, 'wait so long'?" I screamed. I was just here three **MONTHS** ago and was told this..., this..." I was sputtering by now. "They told me this **lump** was only scar tissue from the previous biopsy." Six months before, I'd tried to tell them that this "scar tissue" was growing, but I was repeatedly reassured that it was not, and that everything was normal.

"Never mind," he said, "We've got to schedule another biopsy right **NOW**."

I suddenly realized that the previous biopsy a year earlier had missed the lump. Now may be TOO LATE!

Having breast cancer was bad enough! To find out that the cancer had been growing in my breast for over a year because of the inexperience, ignorance, or arrogance of a doctor was almost more than I could bear.

With eyes brimming over with tears, I was experiencing the worst moment of my life. I wanted to scream, yell, hit out, rage, vent my fury, roll over and die.

"Hey, wait a minute," I thought. "Roll over and DIE?" I was fighting to LIVE. I was going to fight this death sentence with everything I had. And, yet how could I afford to get angry at the very people I was turning to, to help save my life?

If I had only a short time remaining, I needed to get busy. I had a lot of work to do. Thus began my *Race For Life*!

DETACHING ME FROM MY BREASTS

Unfortunately, detaching me from my breasts wasn't that simple. But, it wasn't that difficult, either. When checking into the hospital for the surgery, the nurses who helped me unpack were amazed to see three complete sets of running clothes, three sweat bands, two pairs of running shoes, and not much else. I didn't bother with bras and regular clothing, feeling that I wasn't going to be needing them. They shook their heads as they walked out of the room.

RUNNING TO THE OPERATING ROOM

On the morning of surgery, the head nurse walked into my room with some pre-operative medication, drugs routinely given to patients to relax them and make them sleepy. The bed was empty!

"My God," she said to the nurses aide, "she's run away! And we thought she was taking this so well."

I'd been told the day before that the pre-op medication would be given to me at 5:00 a.m.. I'd set my alarm for 4:00, crawled out of bed, slipped into my running clothes, tip-toed down the shadowy halls, and escaped into the still-dark hills surrounding the hospital.

I covered six miles, enjoying one of the most satisfying runs ever. All the fear, tension, stress, anxiety, and even the anger, seemed to drain away and be replaced by a powerful feeling of being an Army general in charge of waging a war on a battlefield, **my chest**!

The surgeons (four of them now!) were the colonels in charge of the operating room front; the nurses were in charge of the mop-up operations; and the rest of the medical support personnel, with their needles, tubes, and various areas of expertise, were awaiting their call to arms.

At the end of the sixth mile, I was ready to do battle. As I turned back to the hospital and approached the entrance, I was shocked to see my surgeon just arriving. He was even more shocked to see me!

"What in the world are you doing here?" he asked incredulously. I actually felt a pang of guilt, because they would never have given me permission to run if I'd asked.

As it turned out, the staff most certainly would **not** have allowed me to run. When you run, you sweat. Sweating causes dehydration. On the morning of surgery, you can't eat or drink anything from midnight on.

So, here was a sweaty, thirsty, and dehydrated patient "presenting", as they say, to surgery. The head nurse was chewed out for not keeping a closer eye on her charge, and the surgeon told the anesthesiologist to pump some extra intravenous fluids into me to compensate for the dehydration. Under the influence of the numbing pre-op medications, I muttered, "See! No problem with running the day of surgery..."

REACHING FOR RECOVERY

The surgery went very well. I was wheeled from the operating room to the recovery room. As I was coming out of the anesthesia, I was already thinking about doing the exercises that the American Cancer Society's Reach to Recovery support group recommends. Because I was still pretty numb, I was raring to go. As I was trying to lift my arms, the surgeon walked in.

"What are you trying to do?" he asked, looking very perplexed.

"I've got to get started on my exercises!" I told him.

He patted me on the shoulder and said, gently, "I think we can wait a couple of days.

"Oh, OK," I said and immediately fell back to sleep.

The next time I awoke, I **COULDN'T** move my arm. Each time I tried, there were sharp, stabbing pains. I tried for a while to just "gut" through the increasing pain, but then I had this fuzzy series of thoughts: this is only temporary; there's no point in suffering like this; I might as well be comfortable; that's what pain medication is for; and I succumbed to the call of the medication and slept.

The next day I was feeling a lot better and began to wonder when I could run again. When the doctor came by to check on me that morning, I asked him.

"As soon as you feel like it."

"Well," I replied, "when do you think I'll feel like it?"

He chuckled and said, "Oh, knowing **you**, probably in a couple of weeks." He beamed as though he thought that was just **wonderful** news, and I was thinking of all the conditioning I'd lose in not being able to run for two whole weeks.

After he left, I got out of bed and started walking up and down the halls, preparing my body for a possible run the next day.

That night I awoke a number of times, the pain still intruding on my sleep. My body required more medication and more time. The second day after surgery, I was still a little weak and shaky on my feet.

"Damn," I thought, "will I **EVER** get back to running again?" It had been two whole days but it felt like a month!

On the third day, however, I felt great! "Today's the day!" I announced.

I think the poor nurses were in awe of this running-obsessed patient and yet totally supportive. I asked for a wide elastic bandage to wrap around my chest. They brought me a 12" wide Ace wrap which they then helped me swaddle myself so that nothing could move, not that there was much left to bounce anyway. But when the bandages were snug around me, I found I could move with a lot less pain.

Triumphantly, I walked out of the hospital and broke into a tentative, gingerly jog. It felt wonderful! Tears came again to my eyes, but this time they were tears of joy!

ENTER THE IRONMAN!

Part of my recovery was a treat consisting of a visit to my father and step-mother on the Big Island of Hawaii. It was timed, coincidentally, with the running of the 1983 Ironman Triathlon.

Standing on the sidelines of this grueling event, I watched awestruck as finishers completed the 2.4-mile swim, the 112-mile bike ride, and the 26.2-mile marathon.

My brain had trouble handling what it was seeing. It went, "It CAN'T be done!" "Impossible" "Yes, it can. LOOK!" "No, no, no,... no way! **Impossible!**" and so on for hours as the finishers struggled across the finish line.

I'd already run several marathons and knew how I felt upon crossing that finish line — totally spent, exhausted with absolutely nothing left! How could these people run a marathon AFTER having done a bike race which took the average competitor six to eight hours in extreme heat and AFTER a swim which took from one to two hours. It hit me with an intensity I couldn't believe.

As I continued to watch, an idea formed in my head. This time it was "MAYBE I could do that." "No, I can't," "Maybe I CAN," "Forget it, that's crazy," "Maybe if I trained hard enough," "No way, Impossible!" "Anyway, you're too old," (age 48 seemed ancient at the time), "Well, maybe I could just TRY it..." "My God, lady, you're forgetting you're a **cancer** patient!" And that's where it ended...and began.

An image of myself crossing that finish line was constantly on my mind. As I trained, I pictured that scene in Kona, Hawaii: the Timex finish line clock, the tropical flowers surrounding the finish area, the cheering crowds.

I started biking daily and right away began to push the limits of the rides, both in distance and intensity. I signed up for a master's (adult) swim class. I never really "**knew**" that I could do it, wishing I possessed enough "positivity" to do so.

Then came the inspiration. What if I, as a "cancer patient," could complete the Ironman Triathlon! The contrasting concepts, "cancer" and "Ironman" intrigued me. Wouldn't that prove to myself that I really was a survivor and had beat the disease?

What if I took that damning diagnosis of cancer and turned it into the challenge of my lifetime and became an "Ironman" in the process?

What if extreme fitness **COULD** help fight cancer?

What if getting my body the fittest it had ever been was the best offense against the cancer cells that remained in my body? It was an exciting goal, something to wrap my life around, something worthy of a commitment, for surely it would take a large part of my life.

I was "falling in love" with a life with the Ironman. I started getting very serious about all three sports and added weight training. I subscribed to magazines on all four sports, poring over them cover to cover. I bought every triathlon book I could find. I started examining training schedules of every athlete I ran into. My obsession was total.

Then I noticed the physical and mental changes. For example, muscles became defined, and it seemed new ones popped up all over. A friend, Bonnie K., one day looked down at me in mock disgust and shook her head, "You and your 'thirty-year-old' legs!"

I slept like a rock and awakened after five or six hours sleep, raring to go for a morning run, quitting only because I'd run out of time. I ate like a horse and never gained a pound. I felt strong, confident, and as if for the first time, I was really enjoying life.

I'd found a challenge that was totally engrossing and could even forget about the cancer for short periods of time. More importantly, I also felt that I was on to something in dealing with the cancer.

What if there really never would be a "cure"? What if strengthening the body's immune system were the ONLY way to deal with the cancer? I'd asked my oncologist how to build up my immune system. Shaking his head, he replied, "We just don't know."

I developed a theory and it revolved around diet and exercise — to the **extreme**, although I now know is that it's not as extreme as I'd originally thought. I also found it ironic that diet-oriented physicians disagreed with my exercise approach, and exercise-oriented physicians disagreed with the diet approach.

Nobody, as far as I knew, had ever put the two together. It was scary, wading into uncharted waters, but what, after all, did I have to lose?

The body craves movement and when given time to adapt, it can accomplish prodigious feats, even a now 50-year-old body which I'd thought in earlier years was already OLD! I also discovered that there are no limits — only those we set in our own minds.

WHAT ARE THE LIMITS, ANYWAY?

On October 11, 1986 I was sitting in the Honolulu Airport awaiting a flight to take me to Kona for my fifth Ironman Triathlon. I marveled that I was even here since seven months earlier, I was on my way to New Zealand to do an Ironman there. When I won an age-group first place, I thought that I was on top of the athletic world.

That was in March, only five months after I'd done the Kona Ironman in late October. If I were to do Kona again the same year, that would have meant three Ironman triathlons in less than twelve months. I chose to give up doing Kona again and do New Zealand!

After the New Zealand Ironman, when someone asked me what I was going to do next, I wondered if I could do TWO Ironman triathlons in one year, New Zealand and Kona, actually three since it would have been only fifty weeks. (Listen, you get to the point where you count even the HOURS of recovery time! Also, conventional wisdom had it that the demands of an Ironman on the body are so great that a person can only do one a year.)

Then in August, I'd made another choice. It was EITHER the Japan Ironman OR the Kona Ironman in October. I never even remotely considered the possibility of adding another Ironman triathlon in that same year although I was still doing running, cycling, and swim races every weekend.

Since I'd never been to Japan and Continental Airlines had offered to sponsor me, I chose Japan. I fully expected to have to lower my goals as far as my performance was concerned, but to my surprise, I did very well and again placed first in my age group. That's when it occurred to me that my body couldn't tell the difference between racing and training. At this point, however, I still wasn't sure. As long as I gave my body adequate rest time, maybe I could keep racing as frequently as I wanted to.

It never occurred to me that I could do all three Ironman triathlons in the same year! In fact, I was sure I couldn't. People were always telling me I was racing too much, especially my coaches. Since the Japan Ironman had gone so well, I decided to test the limits and do Kona as well. My heart started to race as I realized that all my life, I'd set mental and physical limits for myself.

Who'd have thought that a now-51-year-old "cancer patient" could do four Ironman triathlons in less than one year's time!

That was the training part. Diet also played a key role in my recovery. Shortly after my diagnosis of cancer, I saw a tiny notice in the Honolulu newspaper that read:

"Breast cancer and diet study being conducted. Those who have or have had breast cancer are invited to join a study to determine the benefit of diet in the treatment of cancer..."

I couldn't believe my eyes. If the notice had read "to determine the benefit of cosmic radiation in the treatment of cancer," I would have been on the phone in a flash. I had such a feeling of desperation. Only the slightest hint of salvation is enough to send cancer patients like me into orbit if that's what's promised.

I can easily understand why "quack" cures are grasped at so desperately because that's how I felt. I'd also thought, and been told, that there was no way diet could have any influence on cancer, but here, at least, was hope!

When I got to Dr. John McDougall's office with newspaper clipping in hand, he explained why he thought diet was important to cancer. I learned that the breast cancer rates in countries with a low-fat diet are low. Rates are high in countries with high-fat diets.

So here was the answer to my "why me?" question. The typical American diet of 40% fat is among the highest in the world. Further, when women migrated to high-fat diet countries, their breast cancer rates soon approximated those of their new country IF they adopted that country's diet. In other words, genetics did not seem to play a role. And, neither does age. We are seeing an increase in incidence of breast cancer in **all** age groups.

Even more important to me was the fact that when women in the low-fat diet countries got breast cancer, they lived much longer! This fact grabbed me with an intensity I couldn't believe. Here was hope! Here was a chance to extend my life!

Was there any question about changing my diet? None! Absolutely none!

I was also shown the results of some animal studies which indicated that breast tumors grew much faster in

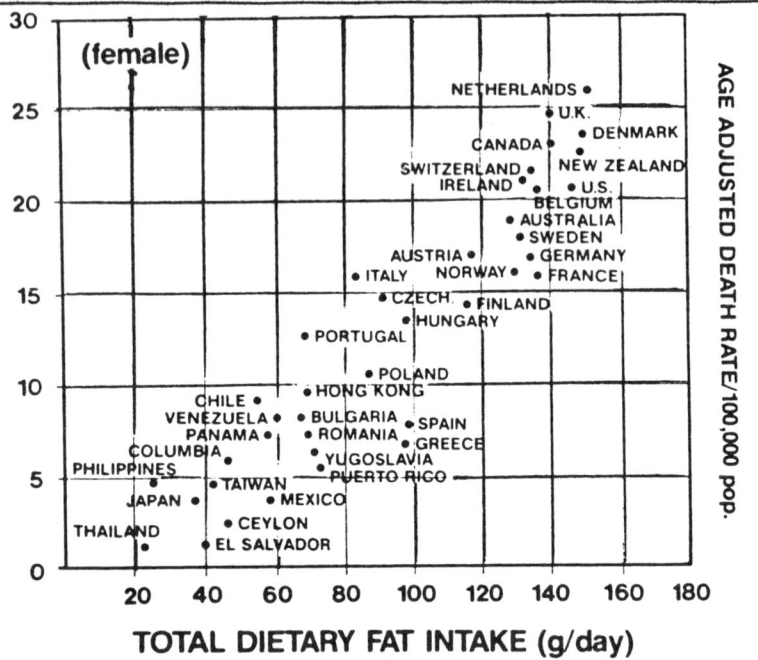

Fig. 1.1 Breast cancer rates are highly correlated with the amount of fat consumed in the diet. (Source: McDougall)

those laboratory animals fed a high-fat diet. For those on a low-fat diet, tumors either grew more slowly, stopped growing, or even, in some cases, fell off.

And that seemed to eliminate stress as a factor, because the "stress" on laboratory animals would have been the same for **all** the animals. And yet there was such a difference in how the cancer behaved.

So, between the population studies and the animal experiments, I was totally convinced and changed my diet literally overnight.

The implementation of the meal plan was easy: *if it's of plant origin, I eat it; if it's of animal origin, I don't.*

My blood cholesterol dropped from 236 mg% to 160 mg% in 21 days, and continued on down to my present reading of 128%, thus practically eliminating my risk of heart attack which I hadn't even considered. Dr. McDougall told me I was at as great a risk of having a heart attack as I was of dying of the cancer.

I was shocked that my cholesterol was so high, since I'd long before given up "red meat" and was a runner. What I didn't know then is that chicken and fish have just as much cholesterol as beef and pork. I had not done my body any favor by switching the source of cholesterol.

The beef and pork industry is fighting back. This is a quote from a 1990 ad in a popular magazine: *"Cholesterol: perception vs. reality. This should make headlines: lean, trimmed beef has no more cholesterol than chicken — without the skin."*

A fast-food chain is now advertising that their "mouth-watering ribs are as **low** in cholesterol as chicken and fish." They must be hoping that their verbal manipulation gets past the public's awareness. "Low" still means "high" in this case.

They've just awakened to the fact that they've been given a "bum rap" for all these years and have decided to exploit this fact.

LOTS OF BENEFITS TO LOW CHOLESTEROL

My new, low cholesterol levels also lower my risk of stroke, colon cancer, and diabetes. But one of the most convincing factors of all was the fact that my race times started to improve. I was knocking off large chunks of time in every race I did. I concluded that my circulatory system had opened up and that my muscles were getting more oxygen and the waste products being carried away faster. I could feel it, and I knew that I was running, biking, and swimming a whole lot faster.

The fourth year after the cancer diagnosis (1986) I ran 51 races and placed in almost every one of them. Thirty-three first places; nine second places; three thirds; and six races that were either relays or "fun" runs with no .

FOOD	CHOLESTEROL (mg/100 G)
Beef	70
Pork	70
Lamb	70
Chicken (Skinned)	60
Turkey (Skinned)	82
Tuna	63
Mackerel	95
Shrimp	150
Lobster	200
Cheese	106

Fig. 1.2. Chicken and fish are just as high in cholesterol as beef and pork.

times or awards. These races ranged from a 1-mile all-out sprint to Ironman triathlons and include numerous course, state, and international records.

In 1987, the fifth year after my cancer diagnosis, I did 52 races, again ranging in distances from the mile to the Ironman, with even more first place awards.

In 1988 I changed my focus a little and ran the Moscow Marathon. Our interpreter there told all the Russians we met about me, a 53-year-old "cancer patient" who does the Ironman Triathlon. I will never forget the looks of amazement on their faces. They wanted to know **everything**: my diet, training schedule, how I got myself to do all these things.

I delighted in the opportunity to talk to these people about the importance of diet, exercise, and a healthylifestyle.

In 1989 I spent three weeks in Thailand and Nepal, doing every race I could find. Again, it was a similar experience. There were many opportunities to mix with the people, share my experiences and tell my "story." People

Fig. 1.3 In front of the Kremlin, the author talking to Russian people about diet, exercise, the Ironman, and Hawaii.

there could hardly believe that anyone would exert any effort that wasn't really necessary for survival.

This was true especially in Nepal where people are so poverty-stricken that it seemed almost criminal to waste any of the body's energy. Food there was such a limited commodity and life so hard that there was no NEED to exercise or select their food carefully. These people already had an extremely low-fat diet and they "exercised" all day long and half the night.

And I saw stress levels that were extremely high. I mentally compared that type of stress with the stress that we in America face with our deadlines, traffic congestion, noise, etc. These people worked long, hard days with no "coffee breaks" and rarely any days off. Even with all this heavy labor, they were not making a subsistence level living. Many of these people could hardly feed their children, much less themselves. Is there any greater stressor than seeing your children go hungry?

Ironically, these people on the average were very healthy and lived to ripe, old, active ages. Obesity didn't exist. Neither did heart disease, most forms of cancer, ulcers, diabetes, osteoporosis, high blood pressure (hypertension), and arthritis. (So much for the theory that stress causes ulcers and high blood pressure, right?)

As a result of the very positive changes in the way I felt and looked, I came to believe that diet plays a very important role in survival, health, and sports competition at any age, and I think was at least partially responsible for shooting me into the international sports arena.

My picture on the front page of the New Zealand Herald the day after my first place in the Ironman there attests to the excitement felt by others. There was a similar reaction in Japan, Russia, Thailand, and Nepal. At last, I, as a "mature" (I no longer consider myself OLD, by the way) female, feel as though I've come into my own. No longer considered an ancient relic to be put on the shelf or rocking chair, but one to be reckoned with in the sports world! Who'd have dreamed it!

CHAPTER TWO

GOAL SETTING: OR, MAKING HARD SEEM EASY

Have you ever watched the buzzing activity that goes on in a colony of ants? Notice how purposeful they seem to be? Each member of the group seems to know where he's going, what to do, and when to do it. Their whole lives are wrapped up in accomplishing genetically programmed goals.

Now look at humans. Some people seem to know what to do, how to do it, and when. I never felt so fortunate. It seemed like I was always looking at a whole bunch of options, wanted more than one, and looked back at the choices I'd made, and wished I'd done something else.

With the diagnosis of cancer, all that got swept away. Suddenly, just being alive was the essence of my life, and everything else was secondary. There came a new and exhilarating sense of reckless abandonment. I wanted to do something really outrageous and exciting.

I looked back at my life and saw where I was one of those ants just following the trail of the ant in front of me. I'd not dared to strike out on a trail of my own making. Cancer did for me what I was unable to do on my own. It plucked me from this trail of conventionality and dropped me in another place, one that seemed so totally unique. Yes, other people have been diagnosed with cancer, but it seemed to me that they were in a different situation than mine. My first two years after the diagnosis were spent assessing the illness, and after it appeared that I was not going to die immediately, I was free to plan the rest of my life.

RUNNING THE GREAT WALL OF CHINA?

I started to think about what I wanted to do before I ran out of time. I felt urges to do things. Travel had always appealed to me and after having been exposed to a lot of travel in my job, I wanted to go places I'd never seen.

Planning a trip to China the year following my surgery, I created and realized a fantastic dream. I ran the Great Wall of China! Well, not the whole length because so much of it is in a state of disrepair, but enough of it to get to experience the feeling of doing something so close to impossibility when compared to my old frame of reference.

Running along that magnificent, ancient creation was a joy in itself, but watching all the Chinese people watching me, was the real thrill. They probably had never seen a tall, blonde, Western female in a running singlet and shorts, and must have thought she was crazy. After all, why would ANYONE want to run when they didn't HAVE to?

Fig. 2.1. Running on The Great Wall of China, Sept. 1983

Waves of people parted and they gawked in awe. They pointed at me, and then smiles played around their eyes, then lips, and then their whole faces beamed.

One almost elderly gentleman playfully ran along side of me, laughing uproariously. He was saying something in Chinese, and I was talking back in English. We communicated soul to soul perfectly, and I know we enriched each other's lives.

TREKKING INSIDE A VOLCANO?

After my return from China, I decided I wanted to backpack across Haleakala, the 10,000 foot "House of the Sun" on Maui. I scampered down the loose rock sides of the inside of the crater of the extinct volcano (hoping the volcanologists were right in their assessment that it really was extinct). I peered down seemingly bottomless crevices, saw two spectacular sunrises, and ran up the far side of the crater in a quarter of the time usually allotted for people to climb out.

As in China, I felt that this was really living, and wondered why I had waited so long to start! I had not yet even **conceived** of doing the "Run To The Sun" where I would RUN the 37 miles from the bottom to the top.

Casting eyes around for another adventure, I thought about the Ironman Triathlon. I told myself that there had to be a limit to what I was physically able to do, and that I did not want to set myself up for probable failure by reaching out for something that was totally unreasonable. And surely, for a 48-year-old "cancer patient," this quest seemed totally ridiculous. This was "validated" by the fact that, as of that moment, no female that old had completed the Ironman. You'll recall we're talking about a 2.4- mile swim, a 112-mile bike race, followed by a full 26.2-mile marathon. I told myself that I had to be absolutely crazy to even contemplate such madness.

During my regular, daily runs, my mind would wander. Images of my getting stronger kept coming up, and from time to time the thought of doing the Ironman would reappear.

Then I recalled my very first road race. It was a three-miler, a Turkey Trot in Springfield, Ohio. It was small enough that I could start pretty close to the front. As I looked around, I could see nothing but males, and I smiled to myself, feeling pretty smug.

IS THIS ANY WAY TO RUN A RACE?

When the gun went off, I was nearly trampled. To avoid getting run over, I ran all out and almost died at the half-mile mark. My chest and lungs were screaming in agony, my legs turned to lead, and I felt as if I were dying. I had no choice but to slow down to nearly a walk. Slowly, I recovered enough to get back up to a halfway decent pace, hung on for the rest of the distance, completed my first race, and collected my first trophy.

I would not forget those excruciating pains for a long time. My next race was over a year later (this was now 1974) and although it was a four-miler, it was essentially a repeat of my first race. But again, I was rewarded with a handsome trophy (no other women, again). Having survived twice now, I entered a 10K (6.2 miles) race and noticed that the same **sequence** occurred no matter what the **distance**.

Races could be divided into a beginning, middle, and end. Beginnings were always great; the end of the beginning was signalled by all those horrible pains in my chest and legs. The middle began as I slowed my pace a little and the pains subsided. The end began as I saw the finish line and then it was trying to just "hang on" until I crossed it. In every race the sequence was the same, except in a longer race, the middle began later and laster longer.

It was four years before I attempted a half marathon. And guess what? The same sequence! By then

I'd had enough experience to realize that any distance I'd tried had the same ending: I crossed the finish line dying, with not much left. The leap from a half-marathon to a full was a greater psychological battle. It was only when I looked around the office and saw guys (this was an all-military male office) with much less training than I, attempting and completing marathons. My rationale was "Yeah, they're ten to twenty years younger than I am, too."

BUT SHE'S TOO OLD TO RUN A MARATHON!

That sexist and ageist argument kept me at that same level for another two years. The breakthrough occurred when I started training with a group of runners with far less training and race experience than I. I decided that I was going to break through those sex and age barriers.

As I crossed the finish line at the end of my first marathon, I realized that I'd gone through the exact same sequence of beginning, middle, and end with nothing left.

Four years later I began to train for my first ultra-marathon (defined as any race longer than the standard marathon distance of 26.2 miles). Once my goal became an ultra, the marathon seemed almost easy. That was an exciting discovery because then I knew that I could set ANY goal, and anything less than that was do-able, almost easy!

That philosophy worked as I increased from a tin-man distance triathlon to a half-Ironman distance, and of course, from a half-Ironman to a full Ironman. In training for my first Tinman, I knew so little about training for cycling, that I thought if I could go the distance, that was all there was to it. It was only after my first opportunity to go "all out" on the bicycle, that I realized that one had to go through the exact same sequence.

This entailed a start, with its accompanying chest and leg pains; the middle, with its backing off enough so I could stand the pain; and the end where the finish line was in sight. That was a major discovery for me (and I suspect most others who were just venturing into triathlons in the early days of no one to turn to and no books to consult.)

Then there was the matter of increasing the distances. Here in Hawaii the shortest triathlon bike leg at that time was 25 miles. The next year, 1983, was the first half-Ironman distance triathlon ever in Hawaii, the Windward Triathlon. I looked at that 50-mile bike leg and wondered how I could possibly go that far. I did it, and then, of course, looked at a 100-mile bike leg and again was totally awed by that distance. Then the 50-miler became "a piece of cake." I have not yet done a Double Century, a 200-miler, but I know that once I set that as a goal, the 100-miler will be easy by comparison.

ARE WE DONE YET?

Another way to slice the training "pie" is to train by time. You can go out for one, two, or say, four hours, especially if you are in a new locale or while traveling. As long as you know that there is an end, and approximately when that end is, you can hang on. What happens when you don't know when or where the end is, is that you want to give up. In the absence of any feedback, your brain says "This could go on **forever!**" and then goes into a state of "overwhelm." When overwhelmed, you are too tempted to quit.

In beginning my distance swimming training, I selected the half-mile course located at the Ala Moana Beach Park near Honolulu. The waters there are warm and sheltered by coral reefs. The first time I got in the water at the start and swam what seemed like forever. Progress seemed frustratingly slow as I picked the high-rise building at the mid-point as my point of reference. It even took "forever" once I got abreast of the building itself. When I finally reached the end of the half-mile course, I WALKED back.

After a couple of months of this, I'd gained enough strength and courage to swim both ways. That, of course, seemed to take the "forever" that the first half-mile did. Interesting, I thought, as I tried to figure out how to handle the longer distances without giving up.

Then I discovered that the lifeguard stands are 200 feet apart and that there are five of them. I knew that it was no problem for me to swim 200 feet because that's only eight lengths of a 25-foot pool. So I do it and go for the second 200 feet or lifeguard stand, and so on.

Now I do 2000 feet so much easier than I ever thought possible. When I get bored, I just count lifeguard stands and it's never more than just a few until the end. That discovery totally changed my concept of the swim distance.

The same principles apply to indoor bicycle training, which, even in Hawaii, is sometimes a necessity or a convenience. Rather than just get on the bike and go for as long as I can, if I just set some intermediate goals, I can get through any length workout.

Another little trick I've learned is to count by tens to a hundred. By counting to ten on each of my ten fingers, I can get to a hundred repetitions relatively painlessly. This is how I get through doing two hundred sit-ups at a time or climbing up a steep hill on a bike while standing. You can always bear the pain a little bit longer when the end is in sight.

1-2, 1-2, RUNNING INTO SELF-HYPNOSIS, 1-2,1-2...

Looking back on my training for the Ironman, I could see that what I was doing was a form of self-hypnosis, although at the time I had no idea of what was going on. First, I'd get into a relaxed rhythm with my running, swimming, or cycling. And, of course, all three of these sports are very rhythmic with their one-two, one-two cadence.

These sports can also be very dissociative. Once you get the mechanics of the running, swimming, or cycling down automatically, your mind will very naturally wander. It was at that point that my mind would start to visualize scenes of triumph and excitement as I could see myself crossing the finish line of the Ironman. What I didn't know then was that I was switching to "right-brain" function.

You may have heard that our brains are divided by neurological functions into right and left brain. The left brain for most people is where we analyze data, have our time consciousness, do our checking of reality; all the concrete, objective types of thinking.

The right brain, on the other hand, is where we create, dream, lose track of time, and are not hampered by **any** practical limitations. We can transport ourselves anywhere in space to any time from the origins of the planet to any time far into the future. We can be **anybody** or **anything**!

It was in this state that I started to transform the dream of doing the Ironman into a reality. I started increasing the length of my training sessions totally lost in right-brain activity. That, of course, also made the training so enjoyable that I'd look forward to the next training session. That, in effect, was the positive reinforcement, the rewards, the nice things I was getting out of my training above and beyond anything I was doing for my health.

So the lessons were learned. As your physical training progresses, your body becomes more able to handle the greater distances. As your body is able to handle more, the mind leads the way by setting greater goals. All you have to do is go along for the ride. And what a ride it is!

CHAPTER THREE

HOW DO WE KNOW WHAT WE KNOW?

Triathletes are among the most sociable people I have ever met. I recall during the early days of running, cycling, and swimming, that my questions concerning the three sports were invariably answered totally, completely, and enthusiastically. The sharing of information seemed to be done so joyfully, and I found that I, too, as I learned the tricks of the trade, felt compelled to share with others.

First, it was to people who asked for help. Next, information was volunteered, as in "Guess what I just found out!" and now, it is shared in the form of seminars and books with the hope of reaching people who never **dreamt** they ever wanted to know all about the joys of running, swimming, and cycling!

As I watched and participated in the sharing of information, experience, and advice, I noticed that there was, unfortunately, from time to time, misinformation that was passed on. Indeed, I had even been a victim of some of these "fads," and it took me a long time to sort out fact from fancy. It's a process, by the way, that is far from ended, as the sport progresses and new equipment, techniques, and strategies are developed and become available to the people training and competing.

Consider this method for keeping elephants out of your back yard. All you have to do is, at exactly 6:00 every evening, sprinkle some pure water over the back gate.

"But," says a friend, "you don't have any elephants in your back yard!"

"See? It works!"

This is an example of superstitious behavior which sustains itself because it never fails to "work." This kind of rationale goes on all around you. See if you can spot some real-life examples of elephant repellants.

A useful way to look at the total universe of knowledge and how it relates to us is to think of four boxes. In the first box there is all we **know that we know**. In the second box there is all we **don't know but *know* we don't know**. In the third box is all we **know but *don't* know we know**. And in the fourth box, all we **don't know that we don't know**.

Most of us are pretty comfortable with operating in the first and second boxes. Much of what we do day-to-day is on automatic because of knowing what we know. Knowing what we don't know usually keeps us from getting in over our heads and out of too much trouble.

All the information in the third box keeps us limited. We don't know what we are really capable of because we never think to test it and, preferably, use it.

The fourth box, however, is where there lies so much potential. There's where the great beyond lies, and where our unconsciousness has never been able to grasp knowledge by itself. It's only when we open ourselves up to what somebody more knowledgeable than we are, that they can take us to realms that we didn't even know existed.

These realms are different for each one of us. It's like living in a forest all your life, never even suspecting there are such things as deserts, mountains, oceans, and space. These poor people may never know what they don't know. Or, take fish, for example. They know all about water but they don't know they know! This is why there is so much potential in the field of self-hypnosis. If we can tap into the tremendous resource of our brain-power, who knows what we can accomplish!

An example of myths and "not knowing what I didn't know" but thought I "knew what I knew." As a child I was told to always wait an hour before going into the ocean to swim. This was, after all, "common sense" because you could get stomach cramps and drown.

As I started my heavy swim training and had to swim hard for 2-3 hours at a time, I found I couldn't sustain that workout without eating first. Then I found out that other hard-core swimmers ate first, too. This told me that the eating-before-swimming-drowning belief was a myth, so I revised my "knowing what I know."

It has been more than thirty years since I've taken my college level philosophy and deductive logic courses. During this time I realized that I could really use a lot of the information I'd gained in those courses that I'd labored through as a college student taking courses primarily to fulfill graduation requirements. Information that previously seemed to have little application to everyday life suddenly was a necessity in sorting out valuable information from mere coincidence.

It was ten years later, while working on my masters degree and a Ph.D, that I was sweating through graduate level statistics and research design courses. It was another ten years before I really realized the value of being able to evaluate facts, hypotheses, raw data, theories, conjecture, trial-and-error, and freak accidents.

What little remained in my head after passing these courses suddenly had applications that I'd never dreamed of. It was like discovering a Swiss Army knife in my back pocket when I'd been limping along using my fingernails as a screwdriver and my teeth as pliers. I marveled at how smart those professors of old were!

I started to see bell-shaped curves and placed people in the middle or ends of human distribution. I started thinking in terms of sample sizes and sampling errors. So what did it really mean if a friend had taken the latest electrolyte replacer and got his fastest ever time. There was also another friend who'd taken the same potion and bonked so badly he had to drop out of the race. So here was one athlete swearing by this product and another cursing it.

When I tried it, I couldn't tell the difference because of the countless variables that varied so wildly I didn't know what was going on. The night before one race I'd gotten an excellent night's sleep but had not had time for my usual pre-race bowl of oatmeal. The next race I'd been up half the night stewing about a personal problem, awakened feeling totally exhausted, but had plenty of time for the usual oatmeal breakfast.

I may have also not bothered to put my fancy 12-spoke racing wheels on, or decided to wear a tri-suit instead of making clothing changes. As I contemplated the almost infinite number of variables, I realized how nearly impossible it was to truly "know" anything!

To really "know" something, I would have had to have two large groups of athletes, one a control group with nothing varying, and the other the experimental group with one, and only one, variable varying. This is the ONLY way to identify the effect of a variable; otherwise, you don't know which cause had which effect.

Can you imagine taking a hundred athletes and, for example, ensuring that they all got eight hours of quality sleep, all had four ounces of oatmeal with apple juice, all wore identical tri-suits, all used identical equipment, all had the same level of motivation to win, etc.

Next, I would have to randomly assign each one to either the control group or the experimental group. Then I would have had to put on a race where the water conditions were identical for each swimmer, the winds the same speed and direction for each cyclist, and footstrikes identical for each runner.

Then I would have to look at the finish times of both groups and calculate the mean (arithmetic average) finish times of both groups, and then determine if the difference, if any, was statistically significant (meaning that it is unlikely that this was a chance variation).

If there was a difference between the two groups, I MIGHT be able to conclude that the electrolyte replacer was the variable that made the difference.

THE PLACEBO EFFECT?

Do we dare to consider the "placebo effect?" The fact that one of the top triathletes recommends a particular electrolyte replacer sets the stage for this common phenomenon of "getting" what we expect to get. The mind is so powerful that it's quite possible that if you're told this little pill will make you go faster, that you WILL GO FASTER!

How can you possibly eliminate the placebo effect when you are trying different foods, equipment, or psychological processes? Why do some people want so badly to believe something that no amount of evidence to the contrary will shake their faith?

This is especially true in the area of beliefs about food. How do you account for the fact that three-quarters of the world's population is vegetarian and yet, most Westerners believe that to be healthy, one must have dairy products and meat? I keep wondering what beliefs I have that are so firmly entrenched that I dare not question them.

What about the people who think if "x" quantity is good, then "2x" will be twice as good, and "3x" will be three times as good? If I ran my best race on 40 miles a week of running, just think what I could do with 80 miles a week, the logic goes. And there are people who, incredibly, run 120 miles a week. The problem comes when some of us try to increase our training mileage to these levels and are rewarded only with injury.

To go back to the example of the electrolyte replacer, if our experimental group was significantly faster, we then need to look at the quantity they drank. Assume it was 24 ounces. What would have happened if they had drunk only 10 ounces? Or 52 ounces? Now you see that we'd have to run another experiment, holding all other variables the same again, and have one control group and three experimental groups.

And are fluid levels of 10, 24, and 52 enough levels to give us the optimum level of fluids? What if 24 ounces is too little and 52 too much?

What if performance increases up to 44 ounces and starts to decrease with greater input? Our experiment with three levels could show that 24 and 52 are the same with our "scientists" concluding that performance does not improve over 24 ounces.

So, another factor to be considered are the number of "data points." Did we go high enough, low enough, or miss the optimum in the middle?

Then, there are lots of arguments for individual differences. Some people assume that we are all basically alike, and others assume that we are so different that we can't learn anything from each other.

The truth lies in between. Within a broad range we humans are remarkably similar, and within a narrow range we are as individual as fingerprints.

As a result, when assessing the outcome of someone else's experimental results, we need to consider whether the results fall within the narrow or the broad range. It's the similarities that allow blood tests to tell us, for example, that our iron and cholesterol levels are normal, or allow surgeons to perform the same basic operation on all of us.

Of course there are differences, and that's why we need, most of all, to keep an open, inquisitive mind, and be very careful about drawing conclusions. Once having drawn a conclusion, it needs to be held in the light of advancing knowledge. Know that when you find you are wrong about something, you are on the way to being right!

CHAPTER FOUR

ATHLETIC SUPPORTERS (AND NON-SUPPORTERS)

Have you ever had the experience of making a resolution to make a major change in your life and then found your willpower crumbling in the face of non-support from the environment?

One of the reasons that formal education is sometimes ineffective is that, although we can change behavior under classroom conditions, as soon as the student goes back to the old environment, the same old behavior appears.

One of the most basic tenets of learning theory is that behavior will recur if it is **reinforced**; and that which is not reinforced will extinguish or drop out. Many people make resolutions to start an exercise program or resolve to start eating better and then find themselves back in the same old habits of not exercising or eating the same old foods.

WHAT? ME CHANGE??

Changing behavior can be considered a two-step process: first, you have to learn the theory; secondly, the changed behavior must be elicited and reinforced. All this means is that we need to know **what** to do, **do** it, and then be **reinforced**. With this powerful sequence, we can control our behavior and make ourselves do anything!

Since this book is about wellness, fitness, and overcoming disease, let's limit our discussion of behavior change to diet and exercise.

In my particular case, I was highly motivated to make a dietary change. After all, as I perceived the situation, the penalty for failure was death. My eating habits changed literally overnight. What then amazed me was that I started enjoying food more.

The most basic foods such as apples, potatoes, broccoli, carrots, and oatmeal, seemed, as if for the first time, to taste so good. I didn't need sauces, spices, sweeteners, etc., to make those foods appetizing. They were already delicious, and I started to appreciate their basic good tastes as if for the first time.

I had learned the theory: that a low-fat diet seemed to enable cancerous animals to live longer. Secondly, the reinforcer was the rediscovery of the good taste of pure, healthful food.

YOU'RE THE ONE WHO'S SICK, NOT ME!

The only difficulty lie in my environment. My husband (Ed. note: now ex-husband) apparently did not see any value for him in eating this way, saying, "You're the one who's sick, not me!" I was even accused of becoming "a religious zealot" in terms of the enthusiasm with which I embraced the dietary change.

Had I not had the negative motivator of fear behind me, I'm not sure that I could have stuck with the change. After all, I could not clear out the kitchen of all the offending foods and had to face the challenge of continuing temptation. I must say, though, that after learning about the problems that meats and dairy products cause, I was not all that tempted.

It was a little different with friends in a social environment. Those who knew of my change were afraid to eat in front of me and thought that I could never find anything to eat at restaurants. I, and they, soon discovered that most any restaurant will be happy to prepare a steamed vegetable platter.

Any ethnic restaurant is probably a safe bet, because their diet evolved from generations of people who obviously survived on that diet.

Mexican restaurants are great because you can order side dishes of rice, beans, and corn tortillas. Note: you may have a choice between corn and wheat tortillas. Wheat tortillas are usually made with refined, white flour, so go with the corn tortillas. This makes an absolutely scrumptious meal and you'll be amazed at how inexpensively you can eat, too!

Chinese and Japanese restaurants already serve fairly healthy dishes. Just go for the noodles and vegetables. More and more restaurants are now serving brown rice. I always ask for it even if I know they don't serve it. I want them to know that the demand is there.

You can also ask them to prepare the food with no added oils, or to skip the MSG if you're on a low-sodium diet. Again, these meals are usually delicious as well as inexpensive.

With regard to making exercise changes, we most always already know in theory that exercise is good for us and most always never get enough. How do we put into practice resolutions to exercise more?

GROUPS ARE POWERFUL STUFF!

One secret I've found is to join a group. This has been powerful stuff for me. First, a group usually has a leader or coach who provides instruction and motivation. Secondly, peer pressure can do wonders in terms of making us want to keep to a task and do it well. The social aspects of groups satisfy other needs as well such as companionship, role models, like-minded friends, and in some cases, compatible lovers.

For about fifteen years I was a solitary runner. I ran the same course, the same distance, the same running form, and did not improve much. Once I joined a formal group of runners who, by the way, were headed by the legendary New Zealand ultramarathoner, Max Telford, my progress was exciting.

I was increasing my distance easily because of the fast friendships which enabled me to run miles painlessly while talking and having lots of fun. We tackled steep hills, bounding and striding up them, laughing all the way. At the end of our workouts, we basked in the good feelings we all had for our training efforts and each other. At races we sought each other out and reinforced each other's efforts.

As I got more into road races, I started to work out on a regular track. Here I was, at the age of 47, learning a whole new vocabulary consisting of "400's," "800's," "intervals," "quarters," and finding out that running around in circles could actually be fun. This group still trains every Thursday evening at the University of Hawaii under the tutelage of the women's track coach, Johnny Faerber.

I miss a workout only under the most dire of emergencies. To illustrate, I recall one Thursday getting off a plane after a five-hour flight from Los Angeles to Honolulu and going directly to the track to run! Even now I do 100-mile around-the-island bicycle rides, get off the bike, and go do my track workouts. This is in spite of being so saddle-sore that I can hardly walk.

Swim training in a pool can be so boring that I could hardly ever bring myself to do it alone. Yet, with a group it is actually fun. Coaches are a necessity here, because swim technique is critical to racing fast, and swim form deteriorates rapidly under fatigue. Even when not tired, it seems that I need constant reminders to keep my elbows high!

The previously mentioned bike rides would never be undertaken alone. In the first place, I always do long rides using the buddy system. It's the safest thing to do in case of accident or mechanical failure. Secondly, a dull, boring ride is transformed into something joyous when riding with compatible people. The experiences we share are so reinforcing that I'm hooked even when not training. And it must work for others as well, since we always have a nice, large, and willing group.

In Honolulu, we also have the OWOW's, the Oahu Wahines on Wheels. "Wahine" is Hawaiian for "female." We meet every Saturday morning to work on cycling techniques and then go for a long ride to build up endurance.

As a fringe benefit we see some of the most glorious sights in the world. We start out by climbing over Diamond Head, go past Hanauma Bay, scream downhill to Sandy Beach and see some of the most beautiful rocky seacoasts on the Island. On clear mornings, we can see all the way to the outer islands of Molokai, Maui, and Lanai. These experiences are so exciting that I keep having the feeling that I wish I could share these with the whole world!

TRY IT; YOU'LL LIKE IT!

Yes, I do try to get people out on the roads or in the ocean. Many have said they'd try it, loved it, and are still out there. A few have said they'd try it, intend to come back and somehow never quite make it, but still loved it. And some will not even try it. Those people in the first two groups are your athletic supporters, and people in the third group are your non-supporters. Surround yourself with athletic supporters, and you won't have any problem maintaining a healthy, fun exercise program.

CHAPTER FIVE

THE DIET: EATING TO RUN, OR IS IT THE OTHER WAY AROUND?

If there is a single cornerstone to this health, fitness, disease prevention and treatment program, it would have to be nutrition. After all, never did my very positive mental attitude and years of running prevent my developing cancer. While a single case does not prove anything, we do see some very convincing evidence in the epidemiological (population) studies where those countries with very high fat diets have very high rates of breast, colon, and prostate cancer, and conversely, those countries with very low fat diets have very low rates of breast, colon and prostate cancer.

Again, this by itself would not prove anything. When you look at the human migration studies, however, you begin to get a pretty clear picture as, within a few years, those people who migrate to countries with a high-fat diet and adopt those dietary patterns, you see rapidly increasing rates of breast, colon, and prostate cancer. Those who migrate and do NOT adopt the high-fat dietary patterns do NOT get those diet-related cancers.

It's pretty clear that this eliminates stress and genetics as causal factors in the incidence of these three common types of cancer. There are a number of animal studies which tend to support these conclusions as well.

This should remind you of a similar situation when the tobacco/lung cancer debate raged. There were those hold-outs who claimed that these very high correlations did not "prove" anything. It took several more years of research data rolling in to convince these people that tobacco smoking did, indeed, cause lung cancer. So where are you going to place your bets?

There are a lot of other convincing factors. For example, when I made the switch to a vegetarian, low-fat diet, I found that, for the first time in my life, my bowels functioned the way they were supposed to. In previous years I could not eat very much in quantity for fear of gaining weight. I was, as a result, always hungry and had rabbit-pellet-sized stools which were brought forth only under great strain. And, I thought, because I'd been told by physicians, that two or three bowel movements a week probably were "normal" for me.

THE CONSEQUENCES OF A LOW-FIBER DIET

It was also very obvious from all the TV and other ads that hemorrhoids were common in this country. Had I weighed and measured the stools of other cultures as did Sir Denis Burkitt, M.D., I would have found out that most of these people had large, bulky, soft stools that moved effortlessly, frequently, and had a transit time (time of travel from mouth to anus) of 8 hours or less as opposed to 36-48 hours seen in this country and England where Sir Denis did his ground-breaking research. I would have also found out that there were entire societies without a single case of hemorrhoids (indeed, they did not even know what they were).

No longer was I plagued with having to worry about being able to move my bowels before a race, or even in some races, with having to make an emergency pit stop. A proper diet actually normalizes the intestinal tract, and I have to relearn this lesson periodically, usually when traveling and I'm not able to adequately control what I eat.

Diverticulosis is another affliction that is common in this country and rare in low-fat, high-fiber diet countries. Diverticula are little outpouchings which occur in the intestines when the peristaltic (muscular contractions) movements do not have enough bulk to "grab". It's rather like inflating a balloon with weak spots. The weak spots in the intestines bulge out and create little pockets. These diverticula are prone to irritation, inflammation, and infection, and can be very painful. When the condition reaches this stage, it's called diverticulitis and, like so many other afflictions in this country, it's preventable.

Amazingly, another **preventable** side effect so many people in this country suffer from is hunger pangs. This is caused from **not enough food in the stomach.** Many people try to control their weight by just eating less, the "push away from the table" method, and therefore, suffer from hunger. The problem is that it doesn't work.

DOUBLE OR EVEN TRIPLE YOUR PLEASURE!

What most people don't know is that they can actually eat two to three times as much food (quantity-wise) and still lose weight! Most plant foods are very low in calories, so one can fill up and feel satisfied on this program.

Since the hunger drive is one of the most powerful of drives, most people who try to deprive themselves soon succumb and will frequently go overboard once they decide "the heck with it" as the body compensates for the period of "starvation." Then come the guilt pangs, new resolutions, and the cycle begins again.

Then, because the body senses that the starvation period is over with and food again plentiful, it starts restoring (re-storing, literally) its fat reserves. It does this as a survival mechanism to get ready for the next period of "starvation." The bad news is that the body gets more efficient at laying in fat stores, and you end up with a higher body fat percentage and a lower lean body mass.

This also means that there is less muscle with which to burn up calories, and one reason why the body puts the fat back on more easily. This is also another reason why exercise is so important; it combats the tendency to lose muscle and will, in fact, add muscle.

This is why low calorie diets don't work. Whenever you start restricting food intake, you are up against this most powerful of survival mechanisms.

If people **only knew** that they could eat as much as they wanted, that they could eat until they were completely satisfied, that they could even lose weight on such a plan, wouldn't you wonder why they don't all do it? Boy, I sure do!

I have all my favorite foods, starting in the morning with oatmeal, bananas, and raisins moistened with apple juice or a teaspoon of blackstrap molasses. This is quite filling and sustains a good early morning work-out or race. From then on, I usually "graze" on whole grain breads, vegetables eaten raw such as carrots, broccoli, and cauliflower, and fruits like apples, oranges, and more bananas and raisins.

Lunches and dinners are always centered around starches such as sweet potatoes, regular white potatoes, sliced and microwaved for about five minutes for instant satisfaction and, one of my all-time favorite foods, plain brown rice.

The nutty, chewy flavor of brown rice is so superior to white rice that I find it amazing that some people still eat the white. Besides tasting better, brown rice is much higher in fiber and the vitamin B complex. I cook mine in an automatic rice cooker, using two-to-one proportions of water to rice. It doesn't even take any longer to cook, usually ready in about 14 minutes. I love it plain or as a base for chili, tomato-based sauce for Spanish Rice, or with water-sauteed chopped vegetables, a quick and easy chop suey.

Dessert is usually a large (I mean like a 4-quart size) bowl of air-popped, plain popcorn. This keeps both hands and mouth fully occupied and has all kinds of positive benefits like lots of fiber, B-vitamin complex, and tastes great once you get past the need for salt and butter.

I have been eating like this for over eight years now. What I've found is that plain, whole, unprocessed food can taste so good. I'll admit that I made the dietary change literally under the threat of death, but I almost immediately rediscovered the wholesome good taste of pure, plain, unadulterated food.

I found my energy levels soaring! Wouldn't you agree that this would have to be the case in order to train for an event like the Ironman Triathlon? I rarely take a day off from training, and when I do, it's usually from the press of other business. I rarely cut short a work-out, and when I do, it's most frequently from running out of time or, once in a while, just boredom.

I sleep like the proverbial rock, and rarely suffer from any kind of depression or moodiness. The most frequent comment I hear from my coaches and friends is that I race too much. I'm delighted when I hear this from "youngsters" 20-30 years younger than I. And, in fact, I do race a lot, as mentioned in my first chapter. I've been doing on the average fifty races a year ever since my diagnosis. That is at least one race almost every weekend all year around. I would do more except that most of the races begin at the same time, 7:00 a.m. Sunday mornings.

TWO-FOR-ONE RACING

Once in a while a novice race director will start a race at 8:00 a.m. This happened twice a couple of years ago. The first time I did the Challenger 10K run at 7:00 and the Civic Center Criterium Bike Race at 8:00. (This was documented, by the way, by "The Hawaiian Moving Company," a local TV series produced by Randy Brandt.)

The second time I ran the Ala Moana 5K run at 7:00, crossed the finish line, grabbed a cup of water, jumped into my car to race across the island to Kailua to do a triathlon at 8:00.

The most exciting part came when I won an age-group first place in both races and both race results were printed in the newspaper coincidentally side-by-side.

Don Chapman, the "three-dot" columnist for the *Honolulu Advertiser*, caught this, telephoned me to ask if, in fact, I had really done and won both races and if so, how, wondering if it was even possible since the races are on opposite sides of the island. Needless to say, I was delighted that he had noticed and the item plus my picture made his column in the next day's newspaper.

BUT WHERE DO YOU GET YOUR...(fill in the blank).

I cite all this as evidence that a vegetarian, low-fat diet can't be all that deficient in calories, protein, calcium, essential fatty acids, minerals, and all those other factors that detractors from this program usually quote.

There is no way that you can be deficient in protein as long as you are eating enough in calories. You will also get all the essential amino acids with a starch-based diet.

You will get enough calcium since you are getting it from the same sources that cows, horses, elephants, etc. get theirs, which is primarily green leafy vegetables.

People frequently say, "But we need SOME fat in our diet." Yes, we do need some, which we get from most every food we eat. For example, lettuce is 13% fat, celery 6% fat, and oatmeal 16% fat. So, the problem is not getting too little fat but one of getting too much.

This also means no added vegetable oils or margarine. You don't need it, and if you add it, it raises your dietary fat percentage to unacceptable levels. Margarine is not a good substitute for butter, because it's been found to raise cholesterol levels, particularly the HDL's, the so-called "good" cholesterol. This is in spite of the fact that margarine has no cholesterol itself.

In order to manufacture margarine, the fat molecules must be converted to trans-fatty acids, a key component of hardened vegetable oils. This formation of trans-fatty acids alters the structure of the fat molecule. All fats, margarines and vegetable oils as well, seem to increase the incidence of cancer. So, it doesn't matter whether it's saturated, monounsaturated, or polyunsaturated: keep your fat percentage as low as possible.

You will feel so much better eating this way that most people who have switched would never go back to the old way. What I have found is that this eating program actually promotes an exercise program. You do more because you feel so good!

WHAT ABOUT CARBO-LOADING?

Carbo-loading is a technique used by some athletes to increase the amount of glycogen, a carbohydrate in the form of sugar that the muscles can use. When you have a hard training bout or a race, you use up the glycogen. You then need to replace it by eating carbohydrates. If you are eating a vegetarian diet, you don't need to do anything different; you are carbo-loading constantly. As a result, you are always ready for anything — training or races in any sport!

THE SECRET TO HEALTH AND FITNESS

I remember one day after completing a 2-mile swim having a "revelation": The "secret" to health and fitness is **what you put in your body and how you move it around** — put in nothing but good food and move it around with lots of exercise. It all seems so simple; every one of the cells in our body has three requirements: nutrients, oxygen, and removal of waste products. The proper diet takes care of the first, and exercise takes care of the second and third!

This chapter on nutrition would not be complete without addressing one of the most common plagues of the Western world: obesity. Obesity is actually a symptom of an improper diet in conjunction with a sedentary lifestyle. There are people who go from one diet to another, or one commercial weight loss program to another. They've spent literally thousands of dollars and still have fat, overweight bodies.

The issue in many cases is cosmetic. This is best illustrated by the popularity of liposuction surgery. With these people, health obviously is not the major motivator. Aesthetics, or cosmetics is.

And this is not to put down the importance of feeling good about how you look. It is extremely important and plays a major role in our self esteem. You just need to know that you can have a beautiful, slim, sexy body by adopting the lifestyle that will give this to you.

Since the majority of this population will at some time in their life go on a calorie-reduction diet to try to lose weight, let's talk a little about why weight-reduction diets don't work, or from another vantage point, why all calorie-restricting diets work — with one great big hooker: As soon as you go off the diet, you'll most likely regain all the lost weight — and then some.

There's no way to beat the system. We humans have, for the most part, pretty strong survival mechanisms. For example, we need oxygen. Now, try to deprive yourself of air. True, you can hold your breath for a couple of minutes, but the drive to breathe will prevail.

Tell someone that they can only breathe with 75% of their normal breathing capacity. Have them come back in one week and tell you how well they did. It would be laughable, wouldn't it? Even if they managed to keep their minds on their breathing during the day, as soon as they fell asleep, they would be breathing full breaths.

Try to deprive yourself of sleep. True, you can stay up one, two, or maybe even up to ten nights, but the drive to sleep will prevail. After only a day or two, the brain will be grabbing micro-sleeps.

Now try to deprive someone of food. Tell them that they can eat only 75% of what they normally eat. They probably will start obsessing about hot fudge sundaes, chocolate candy bars, and banana splits. They probably could stick to the 75% program for a little while, depending on the rewards, but not for very long.

OK, LIMIT YOUR OXYGEN!

Can you imagine a weight loss center saying to you, "Okay, we're going to put you on a restricted oxygen diet. You can only take three-quarters of a breath for the next week. Check back in with us, and we'll see how you're doing." Since you're all motivated, you charge out the door DETERMINED to follow their instructions. How successful do you think you will be?

Well, you're dealing with a very similar situation when you tamper with the drive for food. "Willpower" will keep you going for a little while, but your drive for survival should win. If it doesn't, you risk ending up like Karen Carpenter, the popular, young singer who died of anorexia.

Even if your "willpower" lasts long enough to get your weight down, it will not stay down when you go back to your old eating habits.

Most people, however, will soon chuck the whole idea and binge to make up for the lost food. That's why the whole system of dieting fails, regardless of whether it's a self-imposed, medical, or commercial program. In order to lose weight and keep it lost, you MUST make a lifestyle change, AND this lifestyle change MUST include a change to a low-fat diet along with lots of exercise.

The answer is to let the body eat as much as it wants just as it breathes and sleeps as much as it wants. It will anyway! What you CAN control, however, is what food is available.

A weight control program begins with your grocery shopping. My rule is to shop only on the periphery. Depending, of course, on the layout, you'll find the produce section on one end and the breads on another. So you can go hog wild with the vegetables, fruits, and grains.

IF IT HAS A LABEL OR A FACE, DON'T EAT IT!

Another little rule I have came about as a result of all the admonitions to read the food labels. This rule is: If it has a label on it, don't eat it, or at least, be very suspicious! The label usually means that it's been processed, i.e., had something removed or added. Stick to whole foods and you can't go wrong. Another little rule of thumb I love: If it comes from anything that had a face, don't eat it. So this means what some people call a "vegan" diet — NO animal products whatsoever.

You don't have to worry about food combining because it is impossible to not get enough protein when you are getting enough calories. Nor do you have to worry about getting the proper mixture of amino acids. That is a problem only with carnivores like rats, dogs, and cats. Neither do you need to worry about getting too many calories when you eat low-calorie density foods, which plant foods are. You don't even need to worry about getting enough calcium or Vitamin B-12. We get calcium and B-12 from the same sources that all the other members of the vegetarian animal kingdom do. These vegetarian animals, by the way, have a much longer life span than meat-eating animals do, living more than twice as long.

So, there are so many reasons to eat this way and no reasons not to. Besides, it tastes so good and makes you feel so good. What else could you ask for from a diet?

FOOD TIPS & RECIPES

1. **Beverages**: The best drink in the world is nature's purest, water. It used to be considered gauche to order water as your beverage in a restaurant. Thank goodness those days are long gone. Since I frequently have just come from a work-out, I am usually very thirsty and not only order water, but a very large glass of it. The same is true if I'm at a party, cocktail or otherwise. If I really want to celebrate, I'll have a club soda with a twist!

For variety's sake, there are two other beverages that I recommend. First thing in the morning, as a coffee substitute, I mix one teaspoon of blackstrap molasses in a cup of hot water. Not only is this beverage stimulant-free, but it also gives you a good percentage of the day's allotment of iron and calcium.

The second beverage that I keep on hand in the refrigerator, is a large jug of lemonade — the old-fashioned kind. I buy a bunch of lemons every shopping day and squeeze one into a half-gallon jug of water, adding just enough sweetener to take the edge off. This is a wonderful, healthy thirst-quencher. It is also the only juice I allow myself. In every other case, I eat the whole fruit so as to get all the fiber and the bulkiness that fruit gives. Helps keep the appetite under control, too.

2. **Breakfast**: Six days a week my breakfast consists of oatmeal, cooked very quickly in a microwave oven (2 min.). It does not matter whether it's regular or quick-cooking since the quick-cooking is just rolled thinner. I add raisins, bananas, and a little blackstrap molasses to make a wonderful, filling treat.

For special breakfasts, I make pancakes or waffles using these basic proportions: 2 cups whole wheat flour and 2 cups of water. Add 2 tsp. baking powder, 1 tbs. honey, and 2 tbs. applesauce. If you don't have egg replacer, skip it; otherwise, add 2 tsp. egg replacer mixed with 4 tbs. water. This makes a delicious, healthy pancake or waffle breakfast in no time at all. For toppings, add applesauce or fruit puree. Oh, I almost forgot — please skip the butter. It's not at all necessary for satisfying taste and is partly why such a good breakfast can be so good for you.

This selection also works for breakfasts eaten out. You can almost always find pancakes on the menu. Some of our more health-conscious restaurants out here in Hawaii make whole wheat or buckwheat pancakes, which, of course, are better for you than the standard white flour mix pancakes. Again, be sure to skip the butter and margarine. So, while others may be raising their cholesterol and fat levels with egg-based breakfasts, you can be doing your body a favor and have fun at the same time.

3. **Lunches**: Mid-day meals can consist of any one of many different selections. Some possibilities are baked (microwaved) potatoes with carrot and broccoli sticks, whole wheat pita bread stuffed with sliced mixed vegetables, a whole wheat bagel with an orange and an apple, brown rice mixed with frozen succotash, and so on. This can also make a great brown-bag lunch.

One of my favorite ploys when I'm eating out and something like roast beef sandwiches are being served, is to ask for a "bread sandwich"! A couple of slices of bread along with a salad is adequate, especially if it's a rye or whole grain bread. Whole grain sourdough bread is also sometimes an option.

4. **Dinners**: My last meal of the day may be any one of the options listed above. If I feel like cooking, I make one of the ethnic-type recipes:

Spaghetti made with whole wheat pasta and sauce made with tomato paste, onions, garlic, bell peppers, chopped broccoli, and seasonings, (the chopped broccoli flowerettes can fool you into thinking you've got meatballs, if you're not careful!).

Chili made with kidney beans, tomato sauce, onions, garlic, bell pepper, chili powder, and lots of brown rice.

Pizza made with a whole wheat crust covered with a tomato-based sauce with chopped green onions, round onions, bell peppers, mushrooms, or alfalfa sprouts.

One of the nice things about eating this way is that you can modify almost any of your old favorite dishes. Just skip the animal products, fats, and oils. When you skip meat, increase the vegetables. When you skip oils, increase the water. If you need to stir-fry or saute anything, do it with water. It works very well!

Go to some of the ethnic grocery stores to get ideas for some really interesting foods. For example, a little Thai grocery close by sells a special type of rice, "purple, black or red" rice. They don't know what to call it in English, but it is delicious with its unusual, nutty flavor. And the color really intrigues people who've never seen this type of rice.

Salads are always a healthy selection but can be pretty dull if they consist of the usual iceberg lettuce with a slice of tomato. While browsing through the produce section, look at the variety of cabbages and other greens available. They are usually so inexpensive and make such interesting combinations of dark greens, reds, and textures.

With regard to salad dressings, I long ago decided to skip them. I love salads just plain. For those who can't handle that, sprinkle some vinegar or lemon juice on the veggies.

6. **Grazing:** This is what I do in between meals: I nibble on fruit, carrots, whole grain breads, air-popped popcorn, sweet potatoes, almost anything I have in the house. This goes back to an earlier section which states that healthy eating begins with the grocery shopping. If you keep the high-fat foods out of the house, they can't tempt you. Remember, with this way of eating, you get to eat a lot, eat often, and not gain weight as long as you are exercising, too.

7. **Cost:** One last point has to do with expense. You will be amazed how little this food program costs. Nobody believes me when I tell them how little I spend a month for food. And I walk out with sacks and sacks of groceries because potatoes, cabbage, onions, papayas, apples, oranges, bananas, etc. are very bulky, giving you a lot for your money.

One of the reasons you save so much money is that you are not paying for fancy packaging. This can be one of your contributions to the well-being of the planet by not producing so much garbage. Remember, there's no "away" when you "throw your garbage away." You will be doing your part in protecting the environment from the ravages of our industrial society with its wanton use of resources to make all this packaging available. But, primarily, the lowered cost is in the lesser amount of labor required to process and refine natural foods. And it really doesn't take all that much time to prepare your own foods. You don't need a lot of fancy recipes to make good, nourishing, filling meals — unless you want to.

Oh, yes, another advantage that you will enjoy. Clean-up is so much easier and faster without grease splatters and with no oily film on dishes, pots, and pans.

So how can you pass up such a deal? You can help yourself to glowing good health, save money, and be an "environmentalist" at the same time!

CHAPTER SIX

BODY FAT %: OR WHAT THE SCALES DON'T TELL YOU!

Most people I know are obsessed with their body weight. I hear it in their discussions about food, dieting, weight loss, calories, exercising to burn off fat, etc. You can see it in the television commercials, newspaper and magazine ads, and in the supermarkets. Much of our food industry centers around food that does not do what it is supposed to do, that is, nourish our bodies.

People in this country spend $33 billion a year trying to lose weight. Nearly 75 percent of our population is overfat to some degree, and approximately 50 percent of us are on a diet at one time or another.

At the supermarket you see "low-cal," "lite," "no-cal," and lots of photographs of skinny models or line drawings of impossibly thin bodies. Most people seem to be able to eat more than they burn off. Those excess calories get converted to body fat, much to the dismay of youngsters, oldsters, males, females — everybody! Even a lot of people who don't even look overweight are, in reality, overfat.

This is because the body tucks all those excess calories into muscles as well as the more obvious fat depots along the waist, hips, abdomen, and thighs.

In the last chapter we talked about which foods to eat to provide maximum nourishment to the body which would fill the stomach and not lead to obesity. But for now, it's important to understand the concept of body fat percentage, not body weight. All body weight that is not fat is considered lean body mass, that is, primarily, bone, muscle and water. So, if someone is 15% body fat, they are also 85% lean body mass. (15% + 85% = 100%.)

This becomes important when diet and exercise are considered. A low-calorie diet burns off muscle as well as fat, especially if no exercise accompanies the weight loss. It will also drastically lower the basal metabolic rate, the number of calories used in maintaining minimal body functions.

On the other hand, exercise can help retain the lean body mass while burning off body fat. It will also help keep the basal metabolic rate up. This is especially important to you in the long run, because you don't want your body learning how to become more efficient in hoarding calories.

Take two people, both of whom weigh 150 pounds. One may have a body fat percentage of 5% and the other 50%. In this example, they will look radically different. The 5% will look very lean with good muscle definition, veins obvious through the skin, and contours which suggest a body with very little subcutaneous (under the skin) fat.

The 50% person, on the other hand, will not look at all lean. The muscles will be hidden under layers of fat, no veins obvious through the plump skin, and contours which suggest roundness, obesity, and lack of muscle tone.

These are two extremes. What about people who range from 20-40% fat? What do they look like? Well, a person with 20% fat may look just like the person with 40%, surprisingly. A lot depends on the distribution of that fat. If much of the fat is in the muscles, then that person COULD look quite lean. You cannot tell by appearance alone.

WELL, WHAT *SHOULD* I WEIGH?

What about all those weight tables and charts that tell you what you're supposed to weigh? Well, you already know enough about body fat percentages to see that they and your bathroom scales don't really tell you what you want to know. Don't throw them out yet, though. They are both useful in giving you guidelines and a benchmark to start with.

Since it is unlikely that you will have convenient access to your body fat measurements, your scales can be the first to tell you that you are gaining weight. Now, since muscles weigh more than fat, how do you know which you are gaining? Unfortunately, if you are eating the typical Western diet and leading a sedentary life, we can both bet that the weight gain represents fat. Your clothes will also be providing clues as they get more and more snug!

If, however, you are not taking in excess calories and are exercising at least three times a week for a minimum of twenty minutes (the minimum required to switch your body to a fat-burning mode), you can still show an increase on the scales. This time, however, your clothes will provide the clue. They will fit better, draping over a much sexier torso. If you want to see what your body looks like with no excess fat, look at the anatomical chart of the muscles on the next page. You have all those curves inherently; all you have to do is get rid of the fat that conceals them.

So, how do we know how fat we are? There are more than a dozen scientific methods of measuring body composition. Most of them, however, are limited to clinical and research laboratories, or the meat industry. Unfortunately, the most accurate are the most unavailable and most expensive.

POTASSIUM$_{40}$

Measuring the isotope, potassium 40 (K_{40}) is the most accurate method to date, although there are a number of techniques that are being researched now that have been used to measure animal's body fat. Unfortunately, the K_{40} method requires a lead-shielded room and a lot of very expensive equipment to measure minute amounts of gamma radiation.

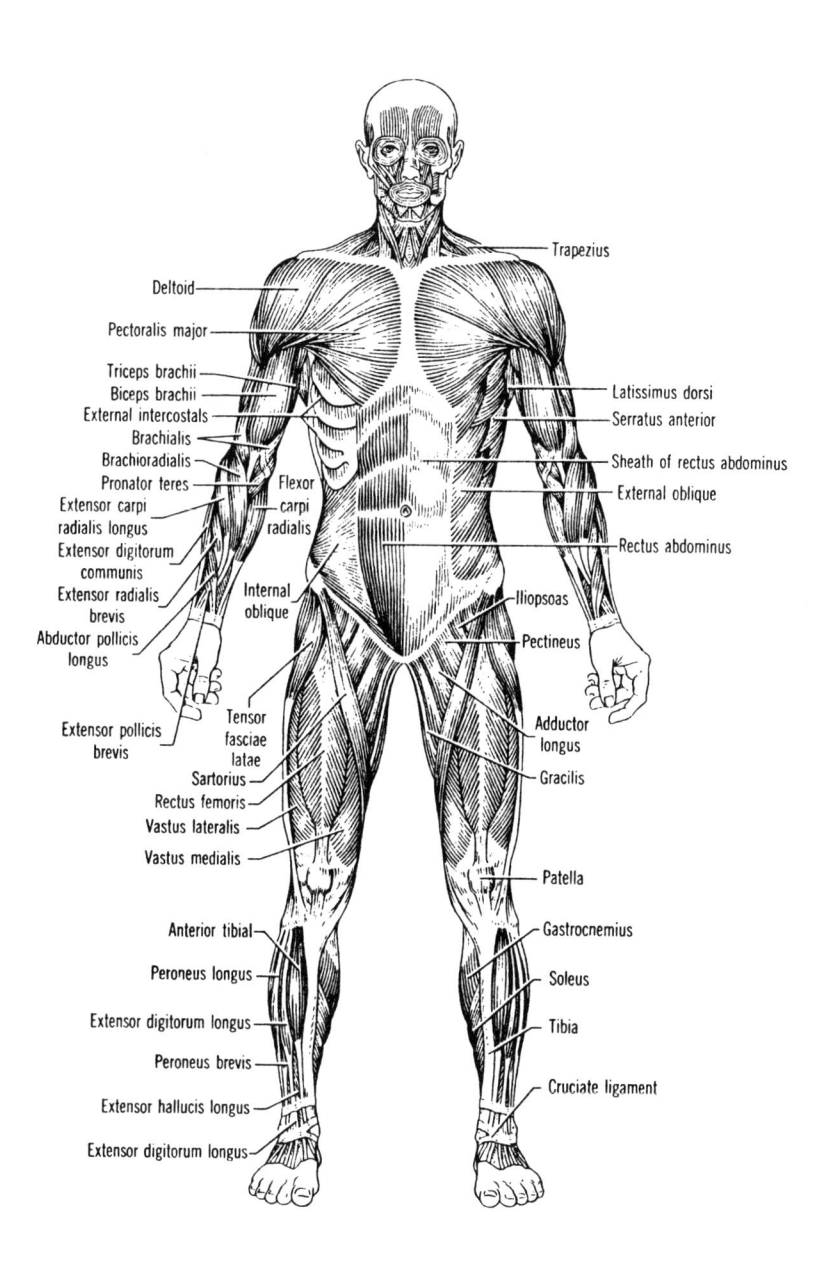

Fig. 6.1 Muscles of the body with the absence of fat.

ELECTRICAL IMPEDANCE MEASUREMENT

Another body fat measuring device estimates the amount of lean body mass by measuring electrical conductivity. This method is convenient, fast, not horribly expensive, (around $20 to $50) but, unfortunately, is not too accurate. Although it's supposed to be accurate to within plus or minus 6 percent, it seems to do a better job of measuring hydration levels in the body (how thirsty you are). The subject is supposed to fast for 12 hours prior to the test, consuming no alcohol or caffeine.

Also, during the previous 12 hours, there should have been no exercise, subjects should not have gone to the bathroom within an hour of the test, and women should not be menstruating. The subject should also lie still for 15 minutes before a reading is taken. The electrical impedance varies depending on whether it's going through lean body mass or fat, and an estimate is based on the measurement of a tiny electrical current passing through the four electrodes placed on the right hand and right foot. It's been popular at some of the running events and triathlons in our part of the country as weight-loss-oriented businesses try to entice new customers.

NEAR-INFRARED INTERACTANCE

One of the newer methods is near-infrared interactance (NIR). A tiny light beam enters the body through a light wand placed on the bicep. The presence of fat changes the spectrum of the light beam. The read-out is quick (about 10 seconds), cheap ($5 to $25), but not yet widely available. The accuracy is supposed to be plus or minus 3 percent and is not affected by previous exercise or hydration levels.

There is a major assumption made in the test, however, that cannot be supported. By taking one measurement (the bicep), it is assumed that the fat percentage at that site correlates highly with total body fat in all people. This is highly unlikely as anyone who has done much body fat testing will tell you.

CALIPERS

The most convenient and inexpensive, but unfortunately, the least accurate method of assessing body fat is the calipers. These look like large pinchers, which is, in fact, exactly what they do— pinch the fat under the skin. This method requires an expensive, well-calibrated set to be accurate, not the cheap, plastic kind usually seen at health fairs, plus a well-trained person to do the testing. The test consists of gathering a fold of skin at anywhere from three to nine sites on the body, measuring their thickness with the calipers, looking up the sum of the measurements of the folds in a chart, and coming up with an estimate of total body fat percentage.

The primary areas of inaccuracy stem from the fact that this method measures subcutaneous (under the skin) fat and not any of the fat "marbleing" our muscles. (You've heard of "marbled steak" as being the most tender? Now you know why!) It also cannot measure any of the fat packed in the abdominal cavity around our internal organs, producing what we in Hawaii call an "opu nui" or large tummy.

Also, people are genetically programmed to store fat in different areas, much to the dismay of the females with their "riding breeches" method of storing fat. The margin of error for skinfold testing is supposed to be plus or minus 3.5% to 5%. The major value of skinfold testing, however, can be in its use as a baseline. Once initial measurements are obtained, you can then implement changes in your lifestyle and re-measure periodically to see what results you're getting. The best, and possibly only, solution to excess body fat is to burn up the fat stores through exercise and a slight but definite deficit in calories.

Well, there is another solution, liposuction, which will work, but which many people feel is rather drastic. Besides being very expensive and being a surgical procedure with its attendant risks, it is highly dependent on the skill of the surgeon doing the procedure. It requires the judicious application of large and small cannulas (suction tubes) which suck tunnels through the fat. It is risky in that you can end up with ridges appearing on the body's surface.

There are other risks as well, such as asymmetry when bilateral (both sides of the body) procedures are done, and flabby, loose skin. There also have been about a dozen deaths reported in association with this procedure. Again, you are much better off using the low-fat diet and lots of exercise program.

Fig. 6.2 Ironman competitor, Alice Unawai, (NZ), getting her body fat percentage tested by the author.

HYDROSTATIC WEIGHING

The last method of body fat measurement to be discussed is the so-called "gold standard" of estimation, hydrostatic weighing. This entails weighing the person under water. The theory behind this method is based on Archimedes' Principle which states that an object immersed in water loses an amount of weight equivalent to the weight of the fluid which is displaced. By submerging an individual on a sling which is attached to an autopsy scale, we can get a weight measurement which determines body density. Through a sophisticated mathematical formula (using regression equations) and the fact that fat has a density of .90 gm/cc and non-fat body tissue (lean body mass) a density of 1.10 gm/cc, we come up with a fairly reliable method of determining body fat percentages.

The disadvantages to this method are that it's not readily available, it's fairly expensive ($20 to $60), and the person has to be able to expel most of the air from his or her lungs while underwater. A lot of people have trouble coping with that. Additionally, a source of error exists in the lungs and the gastrointestinal tract. A very expensive gas dilution system is needed to determine accurately the residual lung volume, and a high-fiber, gas-producing meal can give you a falsely high reading!

An accurate estimate of body fat percentage can be of crucial importance to an athlete. Rapid weight loss by an already lean, muscular individual can cause severe degradation in athletic performance. More importantly, when muscle is broken down, high levels of urea, ammonia, and purines are released into the blood and can cause kidney damage.

Also, when muscle is lost in an adult, it is much more difficult to replace. In a sedentary individual, it will never be replaced and leads to a higher proportion of fat. This, in turn, leads to less calorie-burning tissue, causing the person to gain weight even easier than before.

This is why I never recommend fasting or very low calorie diets. We want just enough of a calorie deficit to cause the body to burn fat, not muscle. And it WILL burn muscle when it is in a starvation mode, or even just "thinks" it is starving. And it will "think" it's starving when it doesn't get enough calories!

This is one of the most critical points to remember whenever you are tempted to try a calorie-restricted diet, no matter how highly acclaimed it is. You can't fool your body. If it's not getting enough calories, it'll start to conserve its reserves of fat. It also gets more efficient at laying more fat stores in when the "famine" is over.

So, how much fat should we carry around? You've probably heard the term, "essential fatty acids," and also heard that we must have some fat to survive. When you consider, however, that the average 30-year-old female is 30% fat, you can guess that there's more than enough here. The average 30-year-old male is 19%, so again, there's lots to spare.

Compare these figures with the average long-distance male runner at from 4-9%, or the female distance runner at from 6-12%. Ironman triathletes tend to run a little higher than runners in body fat, probably due to the fact that swimmers in general carry more body fat.

My own experience is that training bouts lasting 8-10 hours create an enormous appetite, and I had to eat a lot to sustain the energy levels required to complete that many hours of heavy training. I noticed that I could really "pig out" and still be losing weight. The eating part was the most fun part, too!

CHAPTER SEVEN

STARTING A TRIATHLON TRAINING PROGRAM

"Okay, okay," you say. "I'm convinced! I've known for a long time now that I do need an exercise program but I just haven't known how to get started."

Or maybe you're one of those who is an ex-exerciser. You know what to do; you just haven't been doing it.

Or perhaps you're a sporadic exerciser. You go gung-ho for a while and then get away from it. Then when you're ready to start back, you have to go through all the aches and pains of just getting started again.

No matter what condition you're in, the first thing you need to do is plan. In order to plan, however, you need to know your present level of conditioning. If you're a rank beginner, we have to start you at a very low level program. And the ideal program is cross-training, two or three sports that will work out all parts of the body and not overstress any one set of muscles.

GET CHECKED OUT FIRST!

Assuming you're average or normal (and they are not the same thing) and have not exercised in a while, you should get a physician's clearance. This is to rule out any hidden problems that could surface as a rude surprise. This is especially true if you're over 35 or 40 years of age.

A physical check-up would also be a good idea if you're young and have never really exercised, the type who escaped physical education classes for any one of a number of possible reasons and if you have always been an exercise-hater.

Once you've been declared basically healthy and have been cleared to start training, you need to assemble a number of pieces of equipment.

GETTING A RUNNING START!

The easiest sport to start with is running. You'll need a pair of running shorts, a running singlet or T-shirt, and a pair of running shoes. While it is possible to start with "sneakers" and regular sports clothes, it is important to be comfortable and to stay away from possible injuries. Non-running clothes can chafe and bind, and "sneakers" probably will not give your feet the support they need for running.

As you get more into the sport, you can add niceties such as visors, sweat bands, fancy time-pieces to calculate splits and running pace, tights to keep your legs warm in cooler weather, warm-up suits for before and after running, a headset radio to keep you company in areas where it's safe to run with one, water bottles to keep you well hydrated, elastic shoe laces to save you time and effort in putting on and taking off your running shoes, and heart rate monitors that range from ear clips to finger sensors, to straps around the chest that send telemetry data to a sensor at another location.

There are new gadgets out on the market all the time and some of these are very useful. You'll want to evaluate these on your own. You may find that some of them add to the challenge and enjoyment of your workouts.

For the beginning cyclist, things get a bit more complicated. You're fortunate if you already have a bike. You don't need a fancy racing machine to start off with. In fact, it's better to wait a while until you know what you want. For the time being, most any bike will do.

You will probably need some professional help on fitting the bike to you. Adjustments, higher or lower, can be made with the seat and stem heights. I'm afraid NO bike is going to be comfortable for the beginning cyclist trying to go for long rides. You will probably hurt in places you never suspected you'd ever hurt!

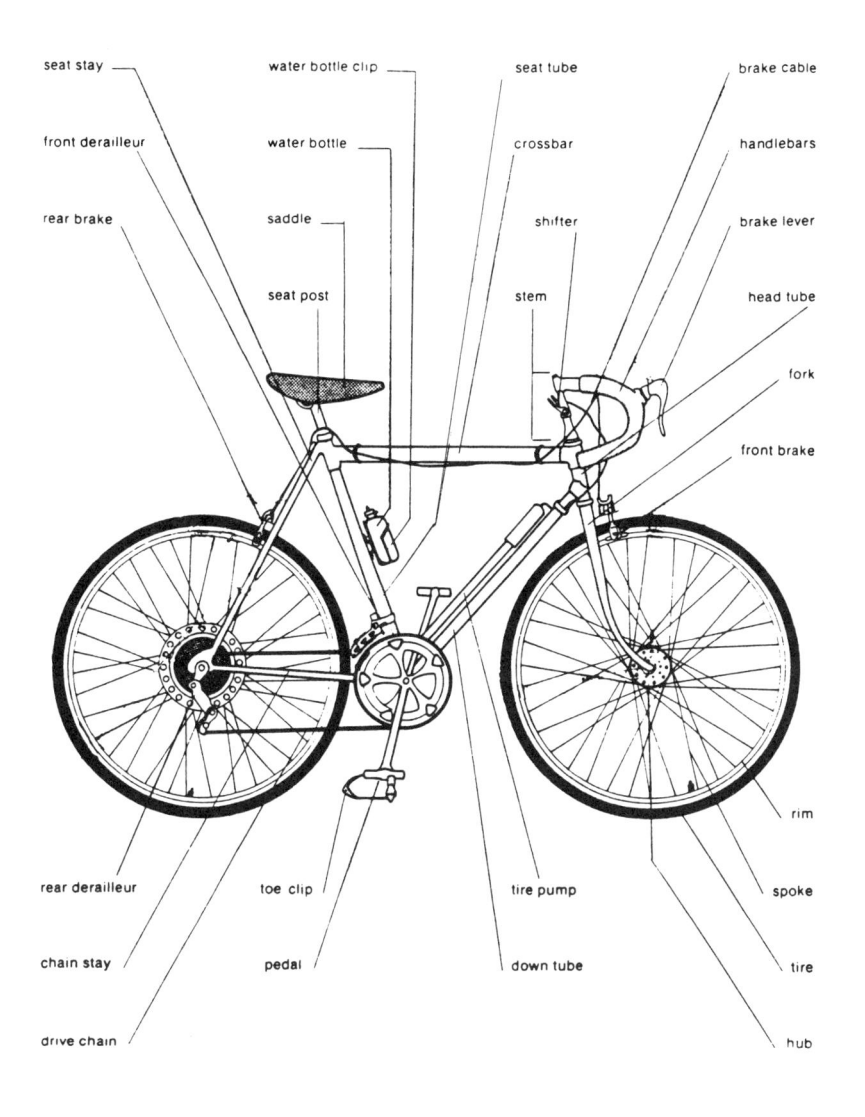

Fig. 7.1 Your "racing machine" with its parts identified.

YOU DON'T NEED A NEW SET OF WHEELS

A few simple modifications will turn any old bike into a pseudo-racing machine. Add one or two water bottle cages to prevent dehydration which is a real danger on long rides. You can unscrew the conventional pedals and add toe clips or clipless pedals which will add immeasurably to your riding safety, speed, and comfort.

A racing saddle won't do much for comfort for a while, but it will be better than the old spring models that a lot of cruiser bikes are equipped with. If the bike has upright handlebars, change over to the racer's drop handlebars.

If you want to go whole-hog, change the gear clusters so that you can do steep hills, add racing wheels to lower your rolling resistance, add the new triathlon style handlebars with elbow pads which put you lower on the bike for a more aerodynamic position, but all these modifications can wait until you've had a chance to see how much you enjoy cycling, how competitive you want to be, and how much money you want to put into the sport.

In addition to the basic set of wheels, you will need a safety-approved helmet. It is crucial that you start out with one since you're most apt to fall early on as you're learning your bike-handling skills. As a matter of fact, falling is a risk that even the cycling experts face because even if you were perfect, nobody around you is. So, play it safe and protect your most valuable asset, your brain.

The rest of the cycling equipment is primarily for comfort. For the body get padded cycling shorts, a cycling jersey, cycling gloves, and cycling shoes. For the uninitiated, a properly-outfitted cyclist makes quite a sight. The shorts are skin tight, have chamois (or simulated chamois) padding in the crotch, and come mid-way down the thigh to protect the inner leg from chafing. Luckily, though, cycling shorts seem to be the "in" thing to wear now.

The cycling jersey is also skin tight and has funny little pockets around in back. After an hour or so on the bike, you'll learn how convenient these pockets are for food, sun block, and more food. The bike should be equipped with water bottle cages, but for really long rides, you'll want to stick an extra water bottle in one of the pockets.

Cycling gloves are funny-looking, fingerless, padded, and colorful. They are fingerless to allow the unencumbered use of your fingers, and padded to help absorb road shock through the handlebars and for when you and the road meet unexpectedly.

Cyclists' shoes come in two versions: touring and racing. Touring shoes look almost like regular shoes except that the soles are more rigid and there are ridges across the center of the soles to hook into the raised portion of the pedals. You can then get off the bike and walk like a normal person.

Racing shoes make you walk funny, just the opposite from tip-toes, due to the cleat which locks into the pedal. These are a little tricky getting used to, but once you've made the conversion, you'll never go back. Implicit in this is another good reason for always wearing a helmet. Novice cyclists (and even some old hands) sometimes can't get out of the cleats in time and find themselves unceremoniously dumped. Embarrassing but survivable!

The next accessory you'll want is for the bike. There are little bags, usually with velcro straps, that attach to the bike under the seat (called the "saddle" by serious cyclists). In this little kit you'll want to add a set of Allen wrenches, a little crescent wrench, a spare tire or tube, a patch kit, some pre-moistened towelettes, and money for a phone call in case all else fails!

GETTING YOUR FEET WET

Swimming requires only a bathing suit and goggles. Most serious female swimmers wear one-piece suits and swim caps, both for aerodynamics, (or is it hydrodynamics?) and males, the non-boxer swim suit and swim caps — for the same reason. Hair, seams, and floppy material slow you down.

Goggles are necessary whether you train in the ocean or a pool to protect the eyes from salt and chlorine, enabling you to see continuously in the water or out. In fact, some of my most enjoyable ocean swims have been off Waikiki Beach where the lava flows from years ago ran into the ocean. You also need to see well above the water line so that you can navigate accurately. So, get good goggles. There's nothing more miserable than hard plastic jabbing you around the eyes, unless it's goggles that fog up. For these reasons, I use foam-padded Barracudas and anti-fog drops. My longest swim thus far has been five miles and while I hurt in a lot of other places, my head wasn't one of them.

There are other miscellaneous training aids which can help allay the boredom of swimming pool laps. These include hand paddles, pull buoys (foam cylinders which go between your legs up at the crotch to raise the lower body and enable you to concentrate on your arm stroke), kick boards (to allow you to concentrate on your kick without having to worry about your arm stroke), and a number of resistance gimmicks, such as a swim suit with pockets like a parachute.

The last two items needed before you start are a watch which can measure seconds, preferably waterproof, and a journal, fancy or simple. You need to be able to record a year's worth of data, such as the time and distance for each of the three sports, the heart rates associated with each, and a column for comments.

CHECKING OUT YOUR PULSE

Now that you've got the basic equipment, we need to do an assessment of where you're at. Start with taking your resting heart rate by counting the pulse at your wrist or neck for one minute. Now, nobody I know has the patience to stand there for a whole minute, so what you can do is count the beats for 10 seconds and multiply that figure by six, or six seconds and add a zero. To get the greatest accuracy, start your count with "zero."

Record this figure in your journal. If you're average, your resting heart rate will be around 72 beats per minute (bpm). Generally speaking, this heart rate will give you an indication as to how aerobically fit you are. The lower the number below 72, the greater the fitness. And, of course, if your heart rate is higher than the average, just think how much improvement you're going to see!

Next, calculate your maximum heart rate by subtracting your age from 220, the theoretical maximum that you were born with. Let's assume that you are 30 years old; your maximum would theoretically be 190. Now, let's calculate your training intensity range. Take 60% and 80% of 190 (multiply by .6 and .8). This gives you a range of from 114 to 152 bpm.

This tells us that anything under 114 bpm is not intense enough to give you a beneficial cardiovascular training effect, and that anything higher than 152 bpm is too intense and that we're courting injury. This training range gives us workouts in any of these three sports that will yield aerobic (with oxygen) benefits, and subsequent improvement in your cardiovascular condition.

The heart rate then gives us the information we need to determine how intensely we should train. The next question is how long. We need to get a baseline measurement which will be determined by how fit you are AT THIS MOMENT. And, your fitness level will vary with each sport.

You will need to find a course to measure accurately swim, bike, and run distances. An example in my local area is the 25-meter pool where I do some of my swim training, a 15-mile route around that area, and a 400-meter dirt track about a block and a half from my house.

To get your baseline measurements, swim four lengths of a 25-meter pool (100 m) and note the beginning and ending time. Later, when fully recovered, bike a 15-mile loop (or some such distance) and note that time. And, again, when fully recovered, preferably on another day, run a mile (four times around a 400-meter track), and note that time. Now you've got some baseline measurements. Also get your heart rate measurements at the end of each of the three trials. These should not be done on an "all out" basis. Do each of these at a comfortable, but not too slow a pace.

It's a little difficult to get your heart rate while doing each of the three sports, but you can stop and immediately get the count to give you an idea where in the range of your heart rate you are operating. You will soon get a pretty good feel for where your heart rate is relative to your level of effort.

If you're rolling along very comfortably, hardly breathing hard, you can be pretty sure that you're at the lower end of 60%, whereas if you're "dying" and panting hard with eyes darting wildly, you are more likely operating at or over the upper end of the training range. You will soon learn when to push yourself a little harder and when you need to back off on the pace.

Some people have difficulty in finding their heart rate, especially if they are swimming or on a bike. According to one of my physician-friends, there is a good correlation between heart rate and breathing rate. What this means is that you can count breaths per minute rather than heart beats per minute. Find your normal breathing rate. This is your baseline and/or fully recovered rate. Then check your breathing rate at the "rolling along comfortably" rate described in the preceding paragraph. This will be within your aerobic envelope, the range at which you want to do most of your training. Don't bother with checking out your maximum, please. That will be past the aerobic threshold and into **PAIN**! We don't want you exercising there until you are superfit and going for age-group records.

You may find that these "trial" distances are where you need to start, that one or more may be too short or too long. For example, you may not even be breathing hard by doing the 100-meter swim. In that case, do 200 or 300 meters. Stop at the point where you feel you are just starting to feel fatigue, measure your heart rate (or breathing rate), and record it. As for the bike, you may just barely be able to get through 15 miles, in which case you can drop the course to 10 or even 5 miles.

The same applies for the running. It may well be that one mile is a good place for you to start. If so, you can plan gradual increases of from 5-10% every other week in all three sports. Then look at your personal calendar and decide when and how many days a week you can devote to your training. For example, you may be able to swim at noon three days a week, Monday, Wednesday, and Friday. You may want to get your biking in to and from work, or Tuesday, Thursdays, and a long ride on Saturdays.

Running may have to be done early in the morning, after work, or whenever. Just be sure not to go more than three or four days between workouts for each sport. Conversely, don't schedule workouts too close together without adequate recovery time. Elite athletes can train twice a day, but most of us mere mortals cannot!

You now have enough information to plan several weeks of workouts. Example: Week 1 might consist of swimming Monday, Wednesday and Friday 400 meters; cycling 15 miles Tuesday, Thursday, and 25 on Saturday; and running a mile early in the morning Monday through Friday. At the end of the week, review the week's workouts and make adjustments, if necessary.

DOING IT RIGHT!

If you are feeling good, strong, and ambitious, you're doing it right. Stay on that schedule for another week. By then you should be ready to increase the distances. So Week 3 might look like this: swim 440 meters Monday, Wednesday, and Friday; cycle 16.5 miles Tuesday,

Thursday, and 27.5 miles on Saturday; and increase the run to 1.1 miles. These gradual increases will allow lots of time for the body to adapt to the new stresses being put on it and will keep you from getting injured. You'll also be developing a triple-sport lifestyle which will make you feel lean, mean, and fantastic.

By Week 4 you'll be able to increase again, assuming that your end-of-week assessments are all still "Go"! Don't be afraid to back off if you are starting to feel soreness or fatigue. But, on the other hand, don't be tempted to jump the schedule by leaps and bounds just because you feel so darned good. That's how many of the "walking wounded" got into trouble!

Speaking of walking, there is a lot of talk about the benefits of walking as a fitness exercise. Naturally, if you are unable, for ANY reason, to run, you will HAVE to walk. What you will find, however, is that walking is not nearly as effective or efficient an exercise as running. It is very difficult to get your heart rate up into the training ranges, and it takes much more time to cover the same ground. As long as you have not waited too long to start your fitness program, I recommend starting with slow running. You'll be miles ahead if you do (pun intended)!

CHAPTER EIGHT

SWIMMING: HOW TO, WHERE TO, ETC.

If you are like me, you learned how to swim many years ago as a child. You may have been taught by your parents, other kids, or through a physical education class at school. My youngest years were spent on Lanikai Beach in Hawaii and I can't even remember learning how to swim. But what I do remember is that I did an old-fashioned paddle-wheel stroke, that is, arms slicing straight down through the water.

Because I learned to swim at such an early age, breathing coordination was never a problem. It's only when I'm coaching new swimmers that the subject of breathing efficiently comes up. There are several basic principles beginning swimmers need to keep in mind.

BREATHING EFFICIENTLY

You inhale between arm strokes in the little trough that forms between your head and shoulder. You pivot your head just far enough to the right or left to get your mouth out of the water, and you inhale on the sideways upturn of the head and exhale on the downturn as your head goes back into the water.

Keep your mouth open and exhale through both nose and mouth. This keeps water out of the nasal and oral passages. Well, most of the time, anyway. Once in a while a wave breaks at just the wrong time and you'll gulp a mouthful. Just figure that you're getting a free sip of fluids and keep on going!

Can you imagine the shock I felt when, as I started to train to do triathlons, somebody told me I needed to "learn how to swim"? Here I'd been on the swim team in high school and had even been a swim instructor and life guard, and now I'm having to learn this new stroke. Not quite as bad as learning how to walk all over again, but ALMOST!

Fortunately, through the University of Hawaii Physical Education Department, Dr. Jan Prins offers a weekend swim video class periodically. I signed up for that and saw a film demonstrating the "proper" arm stroke, which was described as an "s" stroke or like a question mark (?).

In other words, the theory was that you need to keep "new" water moving. The old straight-through stroke just moves the same water and does not move you ahead as fast as when you are sculling from side to side and grabbing new water continuously.

The second day of the course, we were videotaped and shown what we were doing. Then we were taught the new method and videotaped again. What a difference! Although it felt very awkward at first, it was not long before there was no question in my mind that this was a much better way to swim.

The other shock I had was to see how low in the water my legs dragged. Once I saw that, it was no trouble to change my kick and tilt my pelvis so as to keep my legs and feet close to the surface. My swim times began to drop immediately.

So, if you are of the old-, or no-school of swimming, get yourself to a good swim coach and learn the "s" stroke. It'll pay dividends right away.

If you're a more recent vintage swimmer, you're already ahead of the game and will just need to get back into a good training program. In this sport, as in most others, the social aspects can be very important. I always found that training in a group with a good coach was even fun!

EVEN ADULTS NEED TOYS!

In the last chapter I covered the basic equipment required for swim training. I recommend getting the "toys" that go along with swim training such as pull buoys, kick boards, fins, hand paddles, etc. They can help relieve the boredom of swimming laps in a pool, which is where most people have to train.

The ocean is nice to swim in, but most people do not have access to it, and it is almost impossible to measure and time your laps. In this sport, as in most others, the importance of feedback cannot be underestimated. It's that positive reinforcement that gives you joy and pride in your progress, and if you can't measure your progress, you're at sea, literally and figuratively.

There is one disadvantage I've found to doing all your training in a pool. Your back muscles get a rest every 25 or 50 meters (or yards) as you scrunch up to push off against the wall of the pool. Then when you have to do a long swim in a triathlon, your back muscles are unaccustomed to having to hold that same position for the half-mile, mile, or 2.4 miles required in a standard Ironman.

Another skill that you need to train yourself in is to navigate while swimming. You cannot just rely on the black line at the bottom of the pool, because not too many triathlons with open-ocean swims have underwater course markers. I've actually seen it one time; a mile swim course at the Wailea Triathlon on Maui had a line on the ocean floor that traversed the entire swim course!

Barring that, though, it's amazing how many people add a lot of distance to their swim legs by heading off in a different direction from where they intend to go. While you can just lift your head to see where you're going, it ruins your form and speed. You can't always depend on others for your navigation, either. I've seen whole packs of swimmers go off course during a race. If you do get into trouble with navigation, however, your best bet would be to go with the majority.

You may notice, while swimming, that if you have to cough, you'll have a tendency to do it underwater rather than while your face is out of the water, grabbing a breath of air. Your lungs always have some residual air in them. You can NOT exhale all the air from them, even if it feels like it. If, however, you cough underwater, you are tapping into that residual air, which throws off your breathing rhythm and makes you feel as if you need to gasp for air. You may have to break the nice, smooth pattern of your breathing to get more air sooner. This is better than going into oxygen debt. Try to keep as much oxygen going to the muscles as possible by keeping the lungs as full as possible.

If you're doing a triathlon, it's very important to orient yourself at the beginning of the swim leg in ocean swimming. Being off just a few degrees can add minutes and fatigue to the swim leg in a race. Pick a tree, a building, anything that you can see while you're in the water to aim for. Once in a while during a rough ocean swim, the waves can be high enough to make it difficult to see your landmark. That's when you check ahead to see where the other swimmers are, keeping in mind that they may be having trouble, too. Again, in this case, go with the majority until you have evidence to the contrary.

Another little tip to keep in mind when you're doing ocean swim legs in events that have course turns marked by buoys. Sight on the buoys as soon as you can, aim directly for them, and cut the corners so close that you actually brush the buoy. Of course, you may find that a lot of other competitors are doing the same thing. Charge on ahead and get through the choke point as quickly as possible.

A skill that will also help you in navigation, balance your upper body muscular development, and distribute your fatigue is that of bilateral breathing (breathing on alternating sides). Most people learn to breathe on one side or the other and feel that the non-favored side is very awkward. Once swimmers consciously change the pattern of their breathing to alternating sides, however, it soon becomes second nature. As you alternate your breathing sides, you will always know where you are and can make continuous course corrections.

Of course, you do need to keep your eyes open. I would not normally think this an obvious thing to mention until one day I was talking to my favorite training partner, Kate. After her first Ironman distance ocean swim off of Waikiki, I remarked on the beauty of the lava flows through the sand off of Diamond Head and all the beautiful fish we'd passed. She revealed for the first time her fear of the ocean. She had to swim almost the entire 2.4 miles with her eyes squeezed shut!

Katie is, by no means, unique. There are a fair number of brave souls who have to conquer agoraphobia (fear of wide open spaces), fear of sharks, plus normal healthy fear of the hazards of open water swimming. Boats and other over-water craft have trouble seeing swimmers in the ocean. In addition, they are not used to having to look for them.

SWIMMING SAFELY

For this reason, always wear a brightly colored swim cap, and keep a constant watch for all types of watercraft. Always swim with a buddy although there is nothing that precludes both of you from getting run over, as happened off of Waikiki a couple of years ago. Safety is another good reason to develop the skill of bilateral breathing as it enables you to keep an eye on everything around you. Just don't forget to keep casting your eyes about, even behind you as boats and other watercraft can quickly overtake you.

Even if you never intend to become a triathlete, swimming is one of the best forms of exercise. It is excellent training for your cardiovascular system; it stretches you out; and it's gentle on your body. It's a sport you can do for the rest of your life, long after you might have to give up cycling and running.

So learn to enjoy it, and do it as close to daily as possible. If you have a lot of weight to lose, it may be one of the only aerobic exercises you can do until you get your weight down.

AVOIDING BOREDOM

One aspect of pool training that we all have to deal with is the boredom associated with just going back and forth, back and forth. As I'm preparing for a training session in a pool, this thought comes up frequently. There have been a couple of times that I've gone to the pool and been unable to swim, for example, after several of the surgeries I've had when the doctors have not allowed me to swim before the stitches were taken out. Sitting there watching the people go back and forth, I'd think how boring that must be.

Then one day after an enforced lay-off, I got back into the pool, started concentrating on the many aspects of my stroke, responding to the frequent jibes from Ricky, my swim coach, to get my elbows higher, and all of a sudden realized that an hour and a half had passed in a flash! I then understood that what the out-of-the water observer sees bears NO resemblance to what is actually going on under the water!

A WORD ABOUT WETSUITS

Swimmers have discovered that the higher in the water they can swim, the less the frontal resistance. The less the frontal resistance, the faster they go. Well, wetsuits are buoyant and, therefore, keep you higher in the water. So, you will see lots of swimmers in warm, tropical waters as well as the chilly waters of Northern climes, wearing wetsuits. Now you know why. They will also prevent hypothermia, the lowering of your body temperature, too, so at times they are a piece of safety equipment. They are a definite asset to the swimmer's armamentarium.

CHAPTER NINE

BICYCLING: GETTING MECHANICAL

One of the unique things about the cycling leg of the triathlon is that this is the only leg in which failure can be attributed to a piece of equipment. After all, you CAN run barefoot if you lose your shoes; you CAN swim without goggles if a strap breaks or you lose them; but you can NOT do the cycling leg without a functioning bicycle.

For the mechanically disinclined, getting on an equal footing with your bicycle can be pretty intimidating. I've seen young, macho males look at a derailleur and recoil in horror. On the other hand, I've seen "fashion-plate" females with long, red fingernails dig right in with wrenches and come out with the greasiest, dirtiest hands you ever saw. The point is ANYBODY can learn the basics of bicycle mechanics.

The most fun way to learn how your bike operates is to sign up for a course on cycling. In many parts of the country, you can find a course called "Effective Cycling." It's rigorous, well-organized, and sanctioned by a national organization which insures that the course is well taught by licensing their instructors.

Besides teaching bike operation, you also learn what to look for in buying a bike, how to fit it to your body, how to ride in traffic, simple and complex repairs and maintenance, safety maneuvers, bike touring, plus much more. The final plum is that you get to meet the nicest people!

Upon completion of this or a similar course, you will have been transformed into a confident, competent cyclist. You will know your rights on the road and how to merge safely with automobile traffic. You learn things like watching a car's front wheel to know which way and when he's going to turn. You learn "bail-out" maneuvers, panic stops, and even how to fall when all else fails.

CAUTION: BE CAREFUL!

Now, if I've made cycling sound a little dangerous, know that it is. There's no question that there's a great deal of risk involved in placing yourself on the roads where the automobile has been king for so long. Motorists tend to view cyclists as invisible gnats, petty annoyances who belong on the sidewalk or playground, and who have no right to impede their automobile's progress down the road at breakneck speed, if they so choose.

There are even aggressive motorists who, when screaming insults and narrow misses don't seem adequate, will literally try to run you off the road. National and local cycling organizations are grappling with these problems through educational and legislative efforts.

Both approaches are slow and have many obstacles in their way, too. For example, the time to teach cycling is when kids get their first bikes. They are now taught haphazardly and sometimes erroneously. But trying to get cycling into the school curriculum, which is considered by many already overfull, is difficult.

Most people have not seemed to realize that through cycling, kids can learn physical fitness, the basic laws of physics, courtesy, nutrition, independence, and gain a mode of transportation that frees them from the tyranny of automobiles for the rest of their lives. Idealistic, perhaps? But when you consider society's dependence on fossil fuels, the pollution of the air we breathe, and the fact that our kids are growing up obese and very unfit physically, you can see where the lowly bicycle can transform society in some very positive ways.

Here in Hawaii traffic congestion has reach near-panic dimensions. People are having to get up earlier and earlier to get to their jobs on time. People joke about paving the island over with freeways and parking lots, except that it's not a joke anymore! Lifestyles in "Paradise" have been modified to the point that most people would be hard-pressed to see any difference between living in Honolulu and Los Angeles, except that Los Angeles has more bikepaths!

If more people would get on their bikes to ride to and from work and school, they could relieve the congestion on the roads, reduce the need for parking lots, save lots of money, get the exercise/training in during the time they'd ordinarily be sitting in a traffic jam, and arrive at work/school feeling wonderfully invigorated instead of fuming and irritable.

DON'T SWEAT THE SWEAT!

A little sweaty, you say? Just where do I shower, you want to know? That's not a problem! If you start out with clean clothes and eat a non-animal-food diet, your sweat doesn't smell bad. It's the breakdown of animal products that causes the typical meat-eating society's characteristic body odor. And besides, you're using a different set of sweat glands when you're exercising.

We humans have two different kinds of perspiration glands. One set, the eccrine, are those that secrete moisture to cool our bodies and carry off some waste products of metabolism. The fresh sweat of exertion has very little odor. It is only after bacterial decay sets in hours later that you get the typical "locker room" smell, and this is generally from clothes which have not been laundered soon enough.

The second set of sweat glands is the apocrine, the set that does not generally operate when we exercise. It's the apocrines that start functioning when you reach adolescence and that give off that musky, mate-calling scent that we try so hard to mask with deodorants.

So, after your commute to work or school, you can always go to the washroom and take a sponge bath. A quick change of clothes, a comb through your hair, a little make-up if you're female (although you certainly won't need to add that nice, healthy glow to your complexion — you'll already have it!), and you bounce into the office feeling wonderful!

If you're a little fearful about appearing "odd," try to talk some of your work pals into riding with you. Then cycling is absolutely fun, and the bonding that occurs between people while riding gives you a headstart on all your relationships at work. There are all kinds of benefits to be realized!

BEATING GRIDLOCK TRAFFIC

Depending on how far from work you live, you may get all your training in at no extra cost in time. If you get really enthusiastic about riding, you'll be out on the roads on Saturdays and Sundays, too. If that's the case, you'll have no trouble getting in lots of training miles.

If you're like most of us, however, it's a little more difficult getting those miles up to where we want them. Even if you ride to and from work, it still might not be far enough to get the total weekly mileage you need for triathlon training. That's when long weekend rides are a must.

Try to find a bike club with a group of riders who are at or a little above your competitive level. Not only will you get some good training, you will improve rapidly and you will have the safety of riding in a group.

We've discussed training goals in a previous chapter whereby you establish how many miles a week you need to ride, but you also need to look at different types of rides. You can break the rides down into two basic types, endurance and interval training.

Endurance consists of training your legs, heart, and lungs, and, as we say in Hawaii, "okole" (rear end) to hang in there for the long haul. As a beginner, that may be 25 miles, but for the old-timer, that could also be a double century, or 200 miles!

Don't make the mistake that I made in my early days of training. I thought that cycling was just a matter of getting on the bike and pedaling, that I could go on forever that way. I certainly found out differently when, at the end of my first triathlon bike leg, my rubbery legs could hardly support my body, much less RUN!

A weekly long-distance ride will probably handle the endurance part of your training. To take care of intervals, you need to set up a training program consisting of once or twice a week, getting out on a road with little or no traffic, along a pre-measured course, doing a workout consisting of legs of hard cycling, followed by recovery periods. To decide how long and how hard, your heart rate will tell you all you need to know.

CHECKING THE HEART RATE

Start out going very hard for a period of time measured by a watch or cycle speedometer. As your heart rate approaches 90% of maximum, back off until your heart rate drops down to 60-70%. Then repeat the process three or four times. Guaranteed, you will have an excellent workout.

If you don't have a heart rate monitor, it'll be more difficult trying to measure your heart rate the old-fashioned way, but you'll soon get the hang of it as your pounding heart will let you know that it is being pushed. When you can no longer feel it and your breathing starts to approach normal, you can guess that it's time to go again.

If this doesn't sound like a lot of fun, it's probably because it isn't. This is the part of my training program that I have the most trouble with. But this is a case of knowing what to do, not necessarily that I always do it.

We've already covered a little about modifying your old "clunker" into a racing machine and why cyclists wear what they wear. Cycling technology is such that there is a constant stream of new equipment out on the market. It doesn't take long to get on the mailing lists of the mail order catalogs of bike houses so you can see the latest equipment. It's also a good idea to subscribe to at least one cycling magazine to provide periodic updates and receive a monthly dose of motivation.

Because cycling relies on a piece of mechanical equipment which has a tendency to fail on occasion (usually the worst possible moment), view each of your (and your cycling mates') mechanical failures as an opportunity to learn and rehearse what you'd do in a race. If your buddy is an old hand at fixing flats and you're still terrified at the mere thought of it happening to you, you'll ingratiate yourself forever when you offer to change his or her flat.

Don't even mention that, in return for this favor, you expect some tutelage; that usually is never in short supply. Then as you finish getting that rear wheel through the maze of the chain, cog, and derailleur, you'll be unbelievably proud of yourself. What's more, you'll have lost that fear of having a flat under extreme pressure. You'll KNOW you can handle it!

There are lots of other things that can go wrong. As you pile up the bike mileage, you'll be exposed to them first or second hand. Never miss an opportunity to stick your nose into the middle of a mechanical crisis.

Even if you've studied the problem, handled it in the past, you can probably still benefit from the review and help teach others at the same time. You'll feel so much more comfortable on the bike if you know you can handle the common malfunctions that will catch up with everybody sooner or later!

CHAPTER TEN

RUNNING: GETTING FAST & STAYING UNINJURED

Running can be as simple as putting one foot in front of the other and leaning forward. It can also be so extremely complicated that it takes a computer to analyze all that is going on in the body as it moves from point A to point B in a ballistic fashion.

I started running back in the days when there was not a great deal published about running. In fact, it was at a bookstand in July, 1968 that I saw a strangely titled book, "Aerobics" by Kenneth Cooper, M.D.. I'd never seen the word before, so I picked up the book, bought it after thumbing through it, and stayed up all night reading it.

In it I found the definition of aerobic exercise and the influence it had on every body part and system, literally head to toe. At the grand old age of thirty-three, I was plagued with a horrible assortment of maladies. With each chapter that I read, I found a possible solution to a health problem and was anxious to try exercise.

The easiest of all the aerobic-type exercises described in the book was running. It was also the most effective and efficient. It also took no special equipment, and it could be done alone, any time and any place. It seemed ideal for me.

The next morning I went out for my first run (in "tennies," yet) and have been hooked ever since. Learning most everything the hard way means that I've experienced most every injury a body can have, it seems. Since then, I've read almost everything I could get my hands on dealing with running. I've always found the subject fascinating!

How much do you know about running? If the answer is "Not much!," then all you need to know, for now, is to put one foot in front of the other, lean forward, and don't do too much. How much is too much? Your body will let you know. For beginning runners there are all sorts of signals from the body. Foot pains, chest tightness, "shin splints," sore quadriceps (thigh muscles), etc., will be the messages from the body that something new is going on.

At that point, you just back off a little. You don't have to stop; just slow down. You may even need to walk for a while, but do keep moving. Keep track of the time and/or distance covered and be religiously consistent in your program. For starters, schedule an hour a day, preferably first thing in the morning. This way you get it over with, your energy levels will be charged up, and emergencies and/or minor crises will not call a halt to your program.

Now, you will not necessarily be running for the full hour. You will run according to your fitness level and walk to round out the hour.

If you can run for only 10 minutes the first time out, that's okay. Walk for the rest of the time. The next day start again at 10 minutes or whatever level you ran the first day. If things are hurting, stop at 10 minutes. If nothing is complaining, go for 15 minutes. Or if you go around the block the first time, go two blocks the next time.

If you're just starting an exercise program, set your goal for 21 days. Let nothing interfere with this scheduled time, which will preferably be first thing in the morning. The reason for the 21 days is that it takes that long to firmly establish a habit pattern. The reason for the first thing in the morning is that it gets the job done! No interference, no procrastination, and no crisis usually occurs so early in the day.

The main points that must be remembered are: Be consistent and increase slowly! If you do both right, the body will complain a little bit but not too much.

If you're an old hand at running, both principles still apply. I believe every body needs daily exercise, so I'm of the daily school of running, modified in the following way. One day hard or long; next day easy or short. That's why keeping a log is so important. You need to monitor your intensity and distance so that you don't overdo and yet still keep improving.

MAKE IT HURT JUST A LITTLE!

If you keep your body totally comfortable, it could be because you're not increasing the stress on it. And if you're not increasing the stress on your body, you're not getting stronger. So, a little discomfort is a good sign.

BUT, NOT TOO MUCH!

You also need to insure that you don't overdo and get yourself injured. The old rule of not increasing your distance by more than 10% a week or month is pretty safe, when you get to reasonable levels such as a mile or two a day.

The equipment needed was touched upon in the chapter on starting a triathlon training program. The main points to remember are that you need good shoes (good quality with not too many miles on them, but not necessarily anything fancy), comfortable clothing (nothing that chafes or binds), and a source of water.

Running can cause you to sweat a great deal, and it only takes a very small percentage of fluid loss to cause real dehydration problems. This can cause not only loss of performance but also disorientation, possible permanent kidney damage, and lots of things you don't even want to consider having happen to you.

DRINK LOTS OF WATER!

How much water? Remember this little tip: It takes about 8 swallows to get enough fluid in the stomach to activate the pylorus, the valve that opens to let stomach contents into the small intestine. This is where the water starts getting absorbed into the blood stream. Another little test: your urine should be clear. If it's not, you need to drink more water. Remember the 3C's rule: Clear, Colorless, Copious!

If you're an average adult, you probably have a fairly decent running form. Most people's feet track fairly straight along the line in which they're moving. Most people's arms hang loosely from their shoulders and move easily back and forth in rhythm with their legs. And most people are fairly relaxed in their lower arms, neck, and head. If, however, you're not average, you may have some type of running form abnormality. It's always a good idea to find a running coach and have your running stride analyzed.

A good coach can quickly tell you if, for example, your head is cocked to one side, you are carrying your arms too high, or you are throwing your legs out to the side as you run. The real pros have their forms analyzed by computer, although even if you have an abnormality, it may well be that you are compensating for some variation in your body's center of gravity, which is changing constantly as you run.

If this is the case, there will be no need to change your running form. Just be sure to have someone look at you from time to time to be sure that no odd little quirks creep in that could cause you injury or slow you down unnecessarily.

One of the most frequently asked questions is "Don't you find running boring?" And the answer is "Not even close." Besides thinking about the training I'm doing, my mind tends to cover a myriad of things, and I sometimes find that an hour may have passed with my hardly being aware of it. Put me with a group of people, and I am laughing, joking, solving my/their problems, and feeling wonderfully close to them as a result. Sometimes, although not as often, we just run together in silence, just sharing the feelings of our bodies hard at work.

ASSOCIATING VS DISSOCIATING

As your running mileage increases, you will find that your mind either associates or dissociates. This means simply that you stay mentally tuned into your running or you go off somewhere else. I find that I use both. I start a run associating. I think about a slow, gentle warm-up as I gradually increase the heart rate and get cold, tight muscles to gradually loosen and warm to the task. Then I slowly increase the pace but never to a point where I'm uncomfortable.

After a while my mind starts to wander. If I'm bothered by a problem, it'll start gnawing at me and VERY often, a solution presents itself. This is also a wonderfully creative time for me. Ideas keep popping up in my head, so many that I really get excited. Usually, however, by the time I get home, most of them have evaporated. I've taken to running with the micro-cassette recorder that my daughter, Laurelle, gave me for Christmas so that I can capture these ideas. In fact, many of the ideas found in this book were created "on the run", so to speak. I found that if I didn't capture them at the moment, there seemed to be so many ideas that I couldn't remember them all. I've found that there's nothing so fragile as an idea, and nothing so fleeting!

This feeling of being mentally stimulated, being able to solve problems, and having wonderfully creative thoughts has a basis in fact. When we are exercising aerobically, the brain is getting extra oxygen. Not only is there a short-term stimulating effect on the thought processes, there is a long-term effect in the form of increased blood circulation. The brain develops larger, cleaner arteries and more capillary formation. As a result, aerobically fit people think more clearly and creatively.

Another thing to keep in mind is the "talk test." You should run at a speed which is slow enough that you have enough breath to carry on a conversation. If you're huffing and puffing while trying to talk, you're on the edge of anaerobic (not enough oxygen) running and need to slow down.

Running training in general should be aerobic (with oxygen). It's only when you have an adequate mileage base (say, 30-40 miles per week) that you can begin to think about anaerobic training. This would be your intervals at the track, for example.

When you get to this stage in your running training, join a running group. Here in Hawaii, we have several excellent coaches who conduct running sessions at the local high school or university tracks. And I'll bet that most any area has some good coaches, if you'll just look around.

Once you join a group, you'll find that your running will improve dramatically. You will find, first of all, that your enjoyment of running increases, so that alone tends to encourage your running. More importantly is the discipline that a regular session encourages. The structure imposed by a coach and a regularly scheduled meeting time is invaluable.

Coaches are also important information sources. As you increase your running distance and intensity, you may be faced with various aches and pains. It's important to know which ones signal a need to back off in order to prevent injury.

It's also interesting to note that we can tell ourselves something but it never seems to have as much credibility as someone else telling us that same thing. So, get a coach!

Running as an exercise or sport seems to just "grab" some people, while for others, it's a crushing bore. For those like me who love it, the need to increase one's longest run distance seems to be almost insatiable. When you do your first 10K run, you think about 15K.

Then you start to think about marathons and ultra-marathons. Marathons and longer distances, for some, have an appeal that is exciting and challenging.

As one crosses the finish line of their first marathon, they usually think either of two thoughts. One may be, "There, I've done one and I'll never do it again!" Or, they may think, "Wow, if only I'd trained a little better, I could have knocked off ten (or fill in the blank) minutes off my time!"

After a period of recovery, they may start thinking of running marathons in different locales. Marathons are run literally all over the world.

What an exciting way to see new countries and meet people of different cultures who share your love of running. One of the most exotic marathons I could think of was the Moscow Marathon, and it was certainly one of the most memorable. This was before the Berlin Wall came down, when there were still animosities between the Communist countries and the West.

What I found in running through the streets of Moscow, was that the Soviets were intensely curious about Americans, that they were extremely friendly, and usually knew enough English to carry on a limited conversation.

I spent so much time talking to foreign runners during that marathon that I had a terribly slow time, a P.W. (Personal Worst). But do you think that mattered? I was hugely rewarded by being able to communicate with hundreds of people with immensely different backgrounds.

TO RUSSIA WITH ALOHA!

Since I wanted to take the "Aloha" spirit to the USSR, I carried, as part of my baggage, 5,000 Hawaiian orchids which were distributed to the spectators along the course. The expressions of surprise and delight on the faces of the Russians were wonderful to behold.

Even more wonderful were the soldiers from the Russian Army who'd been recruited to serve as course marshals along the 26.2 mile route. They stood at rigid, stone-faced attention. It was pretty exciting to see the stern, cold faces melt into smiles and big eyes as they realized what I was handing them!

Being from Hawaii, I wanted to tell them how far I'd come to run in their marathon. That was when I discovered that they did not understand the word, "Hawaii." They'd just look at me totally puzzled, because there is no "h" sound in their language. When I found out that the Russian pronunciation for "Hawaii" was "G-vai," they all of a sudden understood, nodding their heads, eyes dancing, and big smiles on their faces. Ah, the importance of communication!

There are marathons run in most countries of the world. And I'd like to do them all!

PROGRAMMING THE MIND!

One of the comments that I hear most from people is that they cannot imagine running a marathon as the third event of the Ironman. As a matter of fact, after having done my first 100-mile bike ride, I could not even conceive of **beginning** a marathon the way I was hurting.

The major difference between that first 100-mile bike ride and my first Ironman is mental programming. In other words, when I climbed on the bike that first morning, I "knew" that all I had to do was that 100 miles. That was why I didn't collapse at 50 miles, or 80 miles, or any distance less than 100 miles.

On the other hand, that morning of my first Ironman, I programmed my mind to do a 2.4-mile swim, a 112-mile bike ride, AND a 26.2-mile run. Now, you must have done the physical conditioning to enable the body to support the mind in accomplishing that goal.

I knew, for example, that in spite of feeling intense fatigue at the 80-mile mark of the bike ride, that I still had a marathon to go. I did not give my mind any choice in the matter.

The goal was set. The body had been sufficiently trained to support that goal; and the rest is, as they say, history. As a matter of fact, I have never **not** finished a race. I may have given up on setting any records for a given race, but I've found that I can always dig a little deeper. To me, finishing a race was always more important than anything else, and the positive reinforcement gained from finishing just keeps that behavior going.

I recall at the 22-mile mark of my first marathon, I "decided" that I would never again put myself in that position of such extreme discomfort. About that time a nice, good-looking young male came up along side and started running with me. He, too, was "dying."

Just then, I got an idea. I knew that if we could dissociate for just a bit, we could probably get through that marathon. So I asked him if he wanted to try an experiment to help get us through. He, of course, agreed. I told him to visualize the most exciting erotic experience he'd ever had, or would like to have.

He looked a little surprised, smiled, and said, "I got one!" He shared his, and I shared mine, and the next thing I knew, the finish line was in sight and we sprinted for it. What that taught me was a bunch!

At about that same point in the marathon of my first Ironman, I recalled that experience. I was feeling totally depleted and was wondering how I was ever going to finish. I then dropped back to the person behind me who turned out to be a friend.

DUKING IT OUT

Duke was absolutely miserable! His running shoes had been lost at the transition from the bike, and he'd been offered someone else's shoes in a desperate, last-ditch effort to save the race.

Duke had not only trained hard for a year for this event, he'd also traveled all the way from Saudi Arabia, where he was stationed in the Army, just to compete in the Ironman!

The shoes were way too small, and Duke was bloodied and almost beaten. We started dissociating and, of course, you know the rest. There never was a more welcome sight than that of the Ironman finish line that day!

CHAPTER ELEVEN

PUTTING IT ALL TOGETHER:

YOU'RE DOING A TRIATHLON!

So now that you've got all three sports handled, are you ready to do a triathlon? Well, you could!

These athletic events are so much fun that I think you'll rarely see the competitors without smiles on their faces. Well, most of the age-groupers, anyway. Age-groupers are usually the middle-of-the-packers who are there because they enjoy the sport and want to do well primarily when stacked up just against their age-group peers.

Let's face it. If you're over forty, you really don't have much of a chance against a well-trained 25-year-old. So to keep the action lively for everybody, you get to compete in age groups, usually with a five-year spread, e.g., 20-24, 25-29, 60-64, etc. You will always find male and female divisions as well. So if you get an age-group first place, you know you did very well when stacked up against athletes that are much more closely your equals.

ADVANTAGES OF CROSS-TRAINING

Aside from the fun of the competition, I believe that multi-sport training is better for the body. Each sport tends to emphasize only certain muscle groups. These muscle groups can be overworked, leading to injuries, and leave the other muscle groups under-exercised. Because training is extremely muscle-specific, that is, no other muscles get exercised and trained, multi-sport events cover more of the body. Running emphasizes the hamstring (back) muscles of the legs; cycling, the quadriceps (those bulging front thigh muscles); and swimming, the shoulders, chest, and upper arms. This is not to say that NO other muscle groups get exercised because they do. It's just not with nearly the same intensity.

When you put all three sports together, you get an excellent overall body workout. All three contribute to cardiovascular fitness. And, all three are excellent fat-burners. I've seen bodies totally reshaped into pleasing, curvaceous contours, both male and female. And you can bet that the owners of those reshaped bodies are darned proud of their new forms. Those clinging aerodynamic outfits have more than one function!

So how does the human body cope with all these different demands placed on it? Very well, thank you. Sure, there are muscle groups that tighten up while doing one sport; they get loosened and stretched in another. Blood vessels open up in response to the increased demands made to support the greater blood supply to the muscle groups being used. This happens automatically; and just as automatically, switches to the second, third, or whatever the next set of muscle groups being used.

That's why I have found that it doesn't matter in which order you do your training. Blood vessels are two-way streets, so to speak, and they will shift to wherever the demand is. I have done back-to-back workouts in every conceivable order and have found that the transition is easy. As a matter of fact, although the swim is usually first in a triathlon, I love to end my training with a swim because I'm cooled down and stretched out. The best way to end!

THE IMPORTANCE OF TRANSITIONS

In a triathlon it is obvious that the first one across the finish line wins. What is not as obvious is that it is not always the fastest swimmer-cyclist-runner who crosses that finish line first. Time is required to switch from one sport to another. This activity is called a transition, which at times can make the difference between winning and not winning.

In your workouts you will need to practice transition training. This consists of rehearsing the switching of your swimming gear for cycling gear; cycling gear for running gear.

The best way to do this is to lay out all your equipment in the transition area, thinking carefully about the order of use. As you're coming out of the water, you'll be pulling off your goggles and cap, thinking about what you'll be doing when you find your bike, which, of course, you know by noting the location of a very strategically placed landmark.

Races have been lost because of "lost" bikes. Some triathlons start so early that you're placing your bike in a rack in pitch darkness. When you come out of the water, the scene is totally transformed, not only by the setting, but also by the sea of bikes. Know your bike location!

Want to know how to tell a novice triathlete? They're the ones with the bucket of water to wash the salt or sand off. The old-hands know that it's a waste of time to shower or rinse off your feet before putting on cycling shoes. The salt does not cause chafing, and besides, you will soon be creating a salt bath with your own perspiration.

Don't worry about sand or dirt on your feet from running out of the water barefoot. The sand or dirt will drop right to the bottom of the socks or shoes, and you will never even know it's there.

You know that it's much easier to pull on bike shorts before you put on shoes. Before you put on shoes, you need your socks, if you wear them.

You'll want to pull on your cycling jersey before you put on your helmet. And you'll want to wait 'til last to put on your sun glasses.

All these things suggest the order to place your equipment. You'll also want to have a plastic bag in which to put your swim gear. While the protection of the "used" equipment is not a priority item during the race, the scratching of a $30 pair of goggles can cause a lot of consternation long after the race is won.

Upon returning from the cycle portion of the race, you'll need to dispose of bike shoes (unless you're a supersport who just pulls your feet out of the pedals as you dismount, leaving the shoes still attached to the bike). You can also be pulling off your gloves as you approach the transition area.

Some athletes just run in their bike shorts to save transition time. If it's a particularly hot day or a long run, comfort can be a very important consideration. What have you gained if you've saved 15 seconds in transition and your pace is 5 seconds per minute slower because your body is overheating. Since body temperature rises so fast during exercise, overheating is a real problem. A lot of males also shed their cycling jerseys for the same reason.

READ ALL ABOUT IT!

If you're a serious competitor, you're already subscribing to the sport's journals. This is how you keep up with what's going on in the sport. There have been whole articles on just transitions. These magazines are also the clue to what's new or coming in the field of equipment. Your friendly triathlon shop is probably stocked with dozens of little gadgets (and some not so little) to help you go faster. It's worth your time to do some serious browsing on a continuing basis and be on good terms with the store clerks who very frequently are some of the sport's top competitors.

As you "pick their brains," you'll be picking up valuable tips on all aspects of training and racing. As you find something new and hopefully better, you will need to try it out. It just makes good sense to never do anything different on race day. You will need to literally go through the motions of each transition. When you find the sequence that works best, then you can go through the motions mentally.

Visualization is an excellent adjunct to your training. As you're out on a long run, picture in your mind coming out of the water, how it feels as your legs re-adapt to weight-bearing on a vertical plane instead of horizontal. Imagine how you're going to drink to replenish fluids in spite of not feeling thirsty, etc.

All of this rehearsal will lead to your keeping a "cool head" and not panicking, irrespective of the pandemonium going on around you. I use my transition time to calm myself and run through mental checklists. You will frequently find race volunteers around the area, ready and very willing to assist in whatever way they can.

If you need help, ask for what you need in a very calm, specific way. I've seen competitors yelling, cursing, throwing things, with the poor volunteers saying " 'It?' I don't know what 'it' is! Just tell me what you need". Pronouns do you no good if the volunteer doesn't know which "it" you're referring to. Superstar volunteer, Sylvia Ann Martz, can attest to the importance of this. She has run into this problem numerous times.

In any case volunteers never deserve to be yelled at. They are just as excited as you are and just as anxious to help you get back on the road. Use but never abuse them!

Now, let's assume you've just gotten through your first triathlon. While everything's still fresh in your mind, write down all the "lessons learned." If you're smart, you'll never make the same mistake twice.

Since most triathletes don't do too many back-to-back races, it'll be some time before you do another one. To prevent those feelings of panic the night before a race, make yourself some notes on what worked and what didn't work. It'll also save you a lot of anxiety as you prepare to do your next triathlon.

HAVE YOU HUGGED YOUR RACE DIRECTOR TODAY?

Besides those wonderful volunteers, there are race directors. These self-sacrificing souls also need to be treated right.

If things have gone wrong, the race director needs the feedback, but preferably in a calm, rational way. After all, if it's not a satisfying experience for them, they won't be back either.

So, any negative things need to be broached in a cloak of constructive comment. What race directors love more than anything else, however, is to know what went well with their race. So be a good competitor and treat everybody well!

CHAPTER TWELVE

TIME MANAGEMENT: HOW TO FIT IT ALL IN

Through the auspices of the American Cancer Society's Speaker's Bureau and their breast cancer support group, Reach to Recovery, I've been able to talk to hundreds of people about the value of lifestyle changes in the prevention of, and, if prevention is not possible, then in the dealing with the diagnosis of cancer. One of the most frequently asked questions has to do with finding the time to exercise and eat right.

This issue is one that I faced squarely when I started a running program back in the late '60s. Since I've always been the type of person who gets involved in everything and who has always worked while going to school, time is extremely important to me. In an effort to squeeze more in every day, I've taken several time management courses and read a number of books on the subject. The main principles that I apply have to do with prioritizing things to be done and getting up earlier in the morning.

When I started running in 1968, I was working as a guidance counselor, going to graduate school, and raising and trying to cope with two adolescent kids by myself. As one might guess, any extra time was at a real premium. Yet, after reading Kenneth Cooper's book, "Aerobics," I knew then that I had to find the time to add exercise to my life. It also seemed that adding exercise would not only pay off in physical benefits, but that it would enable me to be more efficient in my work and study.

The only time available to squeeze in my running was early in the morning. By rising an hour earlier, I was able to devote a sufficient amount of time to not only get a good workout in, but I also found that hour was such a wonderful time to be alone with my thoughts. I planned my day, solved problems, experienced the joys of watching a sunrise, felt the coolness and quietness of early mornings, and returned from those runs feeling euphoric, strong, lean, healthy, and hungry.

After a good breakfast, my energy level was so much higher than I'd ever experienced. I knew that I'd found a way to handle all the stress generated from the job, graduate school, and raising kids.

DE-STRESSING "STRESS"

It was in those days that I developed my philosophy of "stress." I feel that "stress" is a catch-all term frequently overused to explain anything that is unexplainable. In other words, it's a scapegoat. What I've found is that when our bodies are exercised strenuously every day, stress as an entity ceases to exist.

Many of the afflictions Westerners suffer are frequently attributed to stress. Heart attacks, ulcers, high blood pressure, acne, insomnia, drug addictions, etc., have all been thought, in this country, to have been caused by stress. Yet, when people eat a plant-based diet and get a lot of exercise, you don't find these health problems.

No matter how pressured I was with the demands of a job that required constant "giving" to other people; the pressures of voluminous reading, writing term papers, a thesis, getting good grades; and enduring the questionable "joys" of raising two teenagers, I still had lots of energy. This could only have been done with an exercise program which allowed me to problem-solve and, at the same time, dissipate the tensions and anxieties that kept building up, i.e., stress. I'd always return home from my runs feeling ready to tackle the world.

HOOKED ON RUNNING!

I was immediately hooked! I integrated running into my daily routine, making it as much a part of my morning ritual as brushing my teeth. Never was there a thought of "should I" or "shouldn't I." I was into running shoes and out the door before I knew it.

To this day, more than twenty years later, I feel the same way about running. The only change has been that I occasionally add a rest day after a hard race. This is only because I've learned that if you don't give the body enough recovery time, it will create it, even if it has to go " on strike" to do it. Rest after a hard effort is just as important as training; just as critical to rebuilding new cell structures whether they're muscle, bone, tendons, or ligaments. I've also become experienced at running through injuries, but that's another chapter.

So, adding running to my daily routine actually bought me time as it added energy and efficiency to my days. But what about swimming and cycling? Well, that took a little more planning.

Since I lived about eleven miles from work and have always thought commuting was a horrible waste of time and gas, I started biking to and from work. I have to admit that, at first, it seemed an almost impossible endeavor. What about showering after? What about change of clothes and shoes? What about make-up and sweaty hair? What about flat tires or other mechanical problems? What about what people would think?

Here I was one of the few managerial-level females who had enough "image" problems as it was! Did I really need to be doing something that could be considered so unconventional? What about that steep hill I lived on and would have to bike down at break-neck speeds and bike up after a long day's labor when I was tired?

HANDLING THE GREMLINS

One by one, I conquered all the gremlins. A sponge bath in the ladies room took care of cleaning up after. I carried a change of clothes and shoes in a backpack. I did my face and hair after arriving at work. I learned a lot about changing flat tires in a hurry, and after a series of flats, learned about vinyl tire liners, (Mr. Tuffy's) which has practically eliminated flat tires from my vocabulary.

I also decided that it was time to give up running my life by what people would think. Then I found out that their reaction was a mixture of incredulity and admiration for the most part. Before long, I started seeing more and more people biking to work.

This is a trend I would like to see accelerate. What a wonderful way to combine fitness and solve this city's transportation nightmare. I even discovered that I could get to work in less time than it took me to commute. There was also the time saved in getting work-outs scheduled.

Getting home was a different story since that hill took a lot longer to climb, but I reasoned that I was getting some "hill training" which builds up power in the legs. I tackled the hill in stages. The first few times I hitched a ride to the bottom of the hill and biked the rest of the way in. On the way home I had to walk the bike up part of the hill only once. After a week's biking, it seemed so natural that I wondered how I could have made such a "big deal" out of bicycle commuting.

Fortunately, the swimming training was easier to solve. There were two swimming pools within a short walking distance from my office. I swam three times a week and in those early days, a half mile seemed like a lot. As my speed increased, I increased my distance. Then on weekends, I did a long (relative to my training level at the time) ocean swim. "Long" used to be a half mile; now "long" is five miles. It's amazing how our perceptions change!

As I started to get more serious about training and competing, I wanted to add weight training. Looking at my calendar, there were the two other noon time slots, Tuesdays and Thursdays. So, weight training got added to the schedule, and I still had evenings free except for the weekly track workouts with my coach, Johnny Faerber, and the "Faerbers Flyers."

When I had my medical leave of absence after my surgery, I relished the additional time that I felt could be devoted to training. What I found out was that when I had more time, I got less efficient and did not get any more training in.

I also found out that the body serves you with a self-limiting alarm. When you try to do too much, it rebels by sending out pain signals. These must be attended to; if they are not, injury is certain to follow.

HOW TO KNOW WHEN ENOUGH IS ENOUGH

So, how do you know how much is "too much?" Other than pain signals, a log or journal is an excellent way to keep track of your training. Book stores carry triathlon log books to track all three sports. I sometimes feel that my training is much like juggling three or four balls; I barely get one ball into the air and another is about to fall. I finish one sport workout and another is almost overdue. The only way I'd know where I stood in each sport is by keeping a running tally in my log.

Another measure I find valuable is my weekly total workout hours. By monitoring this I can pick up trends in my training hours totals (unfortunately, usually downward). By keeping weekly totals relatively constant, I know that the demands on my body are within range. When I need to increase, I usually follow the 10% rule, i.e., don't increase by more than 10% per month. This has served to keep me relatively free of injuries.

People with hectic schedules usually envy those who appear to have more time; they needn't. Busy people are usually more efficient because they **have** to be organized, prioritize their demands, and develop and follow schedules.

I hope that this dispenses with the most common excuse for not exercising. We must find time to exercise, and it will reward us by providing us with more quality time and greater enjoyment of the time we do have.

Scientific studies show that our exercise time investment will be rewarded at the end of our life span: the time spent training is not only added on in terms of living additional years, but also gives us a greater quality of life to the end.

YOU'RE ENTITLED TO 100 YEARS!

The ideal is to live out our full life span (said to be 100 years) with all our capabilities, being completely active, and die in our sleep at the end with little decline in our physical and mental functions.

More than 80 percent of our population dies of lifestyle-related diseases at ages far below 100. It doesn't have to be this way. You have within your power to control your life span through diet and exercise, making drastic changes if you need to. Take a look at some of the masters athletes in their 80s and 90s and you'll see what I mean. They are spry of step, mentally alert, sexually active, and still enjoying life to its fullest. Can't find any of them? Attend some of the World Vets Championship races and you'll see age groups up to and including the 90s. This exercise and diet program really does work!

CHAPTER THIRTEEN

NOT FOR MEN ONLY:

THE SEXUAL ASPECTS OF FITNESS

While walking to the start line of a 10K race at Schofield Barracks one Saturday, I caught sight of Susan, an elite (meaning super-fast) young runner. She, too, was walking to the start line. Along side her was an obviously in-shape, young male. Susan was talking away animatedly and reached out to give him a couple of pats on the behind. I smiled, broke into a little jog, and said as I passed her, "Keep your mind on the race, Susan!" And we all three had a good laugh and an excellent race. (We both won our respective divisions.)

I cite this incident, not only because I smile every time I think about it, but because it illustrates a point. Fitness is sexy. When you feel good about your body, it returns the favor. And when you look around and see a sea of fit, trim bodies, it IS sexy. Bodies without excess fat allow firm, curvy muscles to show through. This is irrespective of the sex and age of the person. We all have the same basic skeleton, the same basic musculature and, therefore, we all have the same potential for beautiful bodies. It's the fat covering up those beautiful muscles that in excess make bodies unattractive.

So it starts with the initial physical attraction. When people run together, they tend to open up and share their thoughts and concerns, many of them very intimate in nature. This creates bonding, a strong emotional attachment between two people. This can happen with people you've never seen before and may never see again. But the bond is there. I can remember people I ran with ten years ago, especially if they were encouraging me at a time when I was sagging and needed it. I know it works the other way around, too, because people that I have encouraged during a race have thanked me YEARS later!

Along with the initial physical attraction and the bonding that occurs with sharing, is the value system that fit people have in common. Athletes value their bodies, their health, their performance, and others who share these values. Conversely, athletes frequently find it difficult to enjoy people who abuse their bodies whether it's by getting fat, using drugs, or just not exercising.

FIT BODIES FUNCTION BETTER!

Besides these psychological aspects, there is the physical side as well. A fit body functions better. Fit bodies have stronger hearts, blood that carries more nutrients, iron, and oxygen, and wide open blood vessels which supply these nutrients every cell of the body.

Some male runners have noticed that they have stronger erections as they get in better cardiovascular shape. This is very likely because as the cardiovascular condition improves, the blood supply to the penis improves. And since erections are a vascular event, it is likely that, as the vascular condition improves, the quality of the erections improve. After all, erections are dependent on a good blood supply.

It also seems to be well accepted that strong erections in the male diminish as they age. The clogging of the blood vessels that supply the penis would explain why this happens. The smart male who values his sex life has another good reason to eat a low-fat diet and get a lot of exercise.

KEEPING A HEALTHY PROSTATE

Another benefit to males from following this program is the very positive benefits to their prostate glands. The prostate is a gland that surrounds the neck of the bladder and the urethra in the male.

As men **in this country** age, their prostates tend to enlarge, frequently to the point where their urine stream is greatly diminished.

In fact, most people, including most physicians, think that this is just an accepted part of men's growing older. This usually meant that older men couldn't empty their bladders completely and, as a result, had to get up during the night to urinate, thus disrupting their good night's sleep.

What's really interesting is that in countries where they eat a low-fat diet, men don't suffer this problem which, by the way, goes by the medical name of "benign prostatic hypertrophy." Doesn't that sound like a good reason alone to eat a better diet?

Then there's also the fact that prostate cancer in men is lower in countries where they eat a low-fat diet. I know this is beginning to sound like a broken record, but what it illustrates is that this is the best diet for **every** reason!

FEMALES DON'T HAVE PROSTATES, BUT...

Since the female reproductive system functions in a similar way (the blood supply to the clitoris, vagina, uterus, etc., is dependent on wide-open arteries, too), this is just one more of the many reasons to take good care of our bodies.

You may have heard that runners suffer from a diminished sex drive, broken relationships, and all kinds of other problems related to increased exercise. This probably comes from the population of runners who are just beginning and experiencing the pain of the initial phases of an exercise program. The condition is soon reversed as their bodies adjust to the heavier stress of the training.

While it is true that anything can be taken to an unhealthy extreme, it does not happen very often in the case of exercise. The greater risk lies in doing too little, not too much. To illustrate, how many people do you know who do too little exercise? Now, how many people have you ever heard of who over-exercise? Most of the people I know are sedentary and are not at any risk of doing too much. On the other hand, I've never met anyone who does too much!

THEN HE WHIPPED OPEN HIS SHIRT...

Because men are subject to some of the diseases thought to be limited to females, I will point out that men also get breast cancer. I will never forget the day that I was talking to Lew P. We had just met and, knowing who I was, said "We have more in common than you think!" With that, he whipped open his shirt, exposing a long, horizontal scar, a souvenir from a modified radical mastectomy. So, guys, breast self exam is for EVERYBODY!

With all the hoopla about getting enough calcium, did you know that men are also subject to osteoporosis? Although they do not suffer the abrupt drop of their sex hormone levels the way women do, the other negative influences of not enough exercise, high protein diets, and the lessening of their hormones all conspire to put men into a negative calcium balance. Luckily, men start out with denser bones which is why they are much older before they start having hip fractures, shortening of their stature, and dowager's humps.

Another point about women's sex hormone levels that you need to be aware of is that they only **appear** to drop abruptly with the onset of menopause. Actually, the levels begin dropping around the age of 35. Some doctors recommend estrogen supplements starting then in order to prevent bone loss. If women are on a low protein diet and get lots of exercise, however, they will maintain their bone mass.

I'll throw out a bit of information that I found absolutely amazing. Did you know that the human female is the only species that undergoes a menopause? All other female mammals maintain an estrus cycle for the duration of their lives. This means that they have ovaries that produce sex hormones and maintain sexual activity all their lives.

I'm not sure what the implications are for human females, but breast cancer patients usually cannot take the female sex hormone, estrogen, so it is academic for me. Female hormones play at least a partial role in many functions of the body, including maintenance of the secondary sex characteristics such as the development of breasts, soft skin, the higher-pitched voice, hair growth rates and patterns, vaginal health, bone strength, healing rates, etc.

Since my doctors fear that giving me estrogen could accelerate the growth of any cancer cells, I am relying on a low- protein diet and exercise to keep my body functioning as close to a lifetime normal as possible.

There are so many good reasons for both men and women to take good care of themselves, but probably the most sexy aspect of fitness is the glowing vitality that a fit person exudes. That, to me, is the sexiest of all!

THE FOUNTAIN OF YOUTH?

Vitality is no respecter of age, and fitness seems to put a hold on the aging process, if not actually reversing it.

There are a number of ways to measure the body's biological age. Among them are strength, speed, flexibility, endurance, blood pressure, resting heart rate, body fat percentage, cholesterol level, and ability to process oxygen. Strenuous exercise along with a low-fat, high complex carbohydrate diet affects every one of these measures. This, therefore, is the closest thing you'll ever find to a "fountain of youth"!

A sad fact is that as people get older, they tend to put on more body fat **even if they don't gain a pound.** This is not sexy, right? Bodies that are lean, muscular, and taut are attractive at any age. The way to fight increasing body fat is to exercise. The fun way to exercise is to train. And the way to keep you training is to enter races.

There is also a role that glowing good health plays on the sex drive. When you feel good about yourself and your body, a natural sex appeal just exudes from your pores. You are attractive to other people, and you'll probably find yourself turned on by other sexy, fit bodies. Wouldn't you like to have a healthy, active sex life until you're in your eighties and even nineties! The old saying "Use it or lose it" definitely applies here.

As women age, they experience symptoms of the post-menopausal period such as the thinning of the vaginal walls and lack of lubrication. According to some authorities, the treatment is continued, frequent usage. Gynecologists can usually tell if older females are not sexually active by the thinning and shrinkage of the vagina. In fact, there is one authority who claims that women should remain sexually active all their lives, even if they have to resort to masturbation to keep their vaginal tissue healthy.

SWIMMING IS SEXY!

A recent study showed that middle-aged and older men and women with regular swim workouts had sex lives as active as people in their late twenties and early thirties. As long as they maintained their fitness program, their sexual interest and activity did not decline with age. Swimmers in their sixties were as active as others in their forties. And not only were the swimmers more active sexually, they were enjoying it more, according to the rating scale.

This makes sense because making love is a physical act where strength, agility, and endurance count. The weak, tired, out-of-shape person cannot hold up very well or very long. Strong, energetic, and fit lovers can throw themselves enthusiastically into lovemaking and last a lot longer. Yes, fit people of any age make better lovers.

In this country, unfortunately, sexual activity is considered an activity for the young and beautiful. Our role models for physical attractiveness are in their late teens and early twenties, so the idea of the elderly engaging in sexual activity is a foreign idea to most people. And it's foreign to the elderly themselves if they are in poor physical condition and feel badly about their bodies.

The other extreme is that of older people still physically vigorous, with strong, supple bodies who still feel good about themselves. They will have the energy and the desire to continue active sex lives as long as they live if they want to. And being in superb physical condition apparently makes you want to!

The apparent reason for this is that the sex drive is dependent on the so-called male sex hormone, testosterone. I say "so-called" because it is present in females as well though in lesser quantities. Studies have shown that physical activity increases levels of testosterone in both males and females and lowers levels of the so-called female hormone, estrogen. Again, I say "so-called" because males also produce estrogen, though in lesser quantities.

This explains why females who train excessively may stop having their menstrual periods. Excessive training in both sexes can have a deleterious effect on the sex drive, probably due to fatigue and a lot less time in their day.

Their sex drive levels usually return quickly when the over-training stops. This resurgence is probably accelerated by the fact that athletes rated themselves as feeling and looking younger and more attractive than other people their same age.

IF YOU KNEW WHAT ALCOHOL DID TO YOUR BODY...

Now, a word about alcohol and its effects on your body. First of all, know that alcohol is toxic to all living cells. Its effects are so scary that if most people knew what it did to their systems, I'll bet they'd stay as far away from it as possible!

Because alcohol is a solvent, it gets to every cell in your body. It then chemically changes the biochemical functions inside every cell. Because drugs plug into the receptor sites on the surface of the cell membrane, they can cause so-called "desirable" sensations (intoxication). They also cause changes in the bilipid (fat) layers of the cells, although there is less damage if you are on a low-fat diet. Alcohol also causes general havoc in cell receptor function and even destruction of receptors.

Your liver has more than 400 different functions, one of which is to detoxify poisons such as alcohol. Unfortunately, chronic use of alcohol knocks off liver cells. Liver enzymes start leaking into the blood stream. Continued exposure to alcohol leads to hepatitis and cirrhosis (scarring). The liver then contracts which causes an increase in blood pressure.

The poor, besieged liver is then hampered in its function to break down estrogen. Since many alcoholic beverages (primarily beer, sake, and bourbon) have a lot of the plant form of the female hormone, estrogen,(phytoestrogen), this builds up in the body. Now, if you're a female, this isn't so bad. If, however, you are a male, this is really bad news.

Your testicles will start to shrivel, and breasts will start to form. In fact, enlarged breasts, gynecomastia, is a telltale sign that physicians look for in checking for alcoholism. Males then become impotent, fertility is impaired, and both males and females suffer loss of libido (sex drive) and become anorgasmic (inability to have an orgasm). If you value your sexuality, you sure have enough reasons to stay away from alcohol.

So, you see, there's a lot more to glowing, good health than most people realize. Fitness is sexy and if you're fit enough to do triathlons, you'll probably be in top sexual form as well. Triathlons are sexy for several reasons, and now you know what triathletes are referring to when they talk about the fourth event!

CHAPTER FOURTEEN
ANEMIA AND THE BOSTON MARATHON

One of the more interesting aspects of my journey to become an Ironman has been the opportunity to learn a lot about my body and human bodies in general. As I increased my training levels in running by doing ultramarathons (any run greater than a marathon, 26.2 miles), I started to notice increasing fatigue. Normal, you say? No, not in this case.

Besides increasing fatigue, I noticed that after a long, hard run or race, I experienced light-headedness. Right after crossing the finish line of my first 50 kilometer race, I nearly passed out. Knowing enough to get my head down, I headed for the curb of the street and quickly got my head between my knees.

My thoughts at this time were, "Wow, guess I'm really pushing my limits!" I felt that this reaction was normal and of no real concern. When I went to stand up again a few minutes later, however, I nearly passed out again. I started to get a little concerned since it was then close to midnight, and I had to drive myself home.

Somebody brought me some food and drink which I quickly downed, thinking that my blood sugar must be too low. After a few more minutes, I felt much better. I climbed in my car and made it home and to bed.

The next morning when I awakened, I still felt light-headed. Furthermore, I discovered I had "melena," black, tarry stools. This is the hallmark of GI (gastrointestinal) bleeding. I called the Emergency Room of the now-very-familiar Tripler Hospital and described the symptoms, asking if this was of any real concern. When they said to get myself "immediately in the hands of competent medical care," I decided that it must be serious.

This happened in 1984 when most medical personnel did not know a great deal about some of the maladies that affect long-distance runners. These symptoms could be life-threatening, they emphasized.

One of the first things they did was to try to put a nasogastric (NG) tube into my stomach. Of all the medical procedures I've ever had done, this was by far the most unpleasant. It involved sticking a K-Y-jellied tube into a nostril, trying to miss the trachea while aiming for the esophagus. You probably know that the trachea leads to the lungs and, if blocked, makes it impossible to breathe—a feeling that causes extreme panic.

Well, wouldn't you guess that it was my trachea they hit! With the tube totally blocking the entrance to the trachea, I started gagging and struggled to breathe. Panicking, I started to swing wildly. They quickly pulled the tube out and apologized profusely. They said they needed to try again, but I was too shaken.

The experience was so unpleasant that I refused to let them try again. No amount of pleading was going to change my mind, so they brought in some reinforcements. The chief of the ER said that I could be bleeding to death and that this was the only way to see what was going on.

YOU COULD BE BLEEDING TO DEATH!

I told him that I was sure I wasn't bleeding to death, and, besides, I had to leave to get to my track workout. The doctor looked aghast!

"You're not going anywhere! You don't seem to realize the seriousness of the situation. We are going to have to hospitalize you. We **must** find the source of the bleeding. Now, I know what you just went through was extremely unpleasant, but we've got more experienced people who will not miss this time."

I was in turmoil. I sat there for a long time trying to reason things out. If they were right, I would need to consent to them trying the procedure again. I thought then about the faintness and melena. Then those panicky feelings would recreate themselves. He let me wade through the pros and cons for a while.

"I will do my best to minimize the discomfort; we've got to find the source of the bleeding."

I resigned myself to what seemed to be the inevitable. This time he did hit the esophagus and fed the tube into the stomach. Attaching a syringe to the end of the tube, he started aspirating the contents of my stomach. In spite of the discomfort of a tube through my nose and down my throat and into my stomach, I watched wide-eyed, intrigued by what was going on. What was coming out of my stomach looked like coffee grounds.

"Uh-oh," they said. "That's bad news; you're bleeding from the stomach. There'll be no track work-out today. We're keeping you right here!"

Instead of my life passing before my eyes, a vision of my next race, the Boston Marathon, and the Ironman went flying by. When the results of my blood tests came back from the lab, I was told that I was extremely anemic. My hemoglobin was 6.8; hematocrit 24; TIBC 399; and serum ferritin 6. What all this meant was that, according to the doctor, I should be flat on my back getting a transfusion. (See Appendix 1 for an explanation of the laboratory tests.)

The situation was serious. I was supposed to be getting on a plane in two days to do the Boston Marathon! All you serious runners know that Boston is the Holy Grail of runners. I had worked too hard to qualify for Boston and was not giving it up easily.

I begged; I pleaded!

"Look," I said, "I just finished a 50-kilometer run. If I were in as bad shape as you say, I wouldn't have been able to do that."

The doctor shook his head. "I don't know how you did it, but you are risking damage to your heart muscle by insisting on doing this. Being this anemic, your blood can't carry enough oxygen to support the demands of a marathon on your heart. You're crazy to even consider it."

I felt convinced. After all, I was doing this for fitness; it didn't make sense to create damage to my heart while trying to get stronger. I missed my track workout, and got to spend the night in the "Tripler Hotel."

HEALED IN TWENTY-FOUR HOURS!

The next day I was "scoped." This means an endoscope was passed into my stomach and upper intestine to let the doctors see what condition my GI tract was in. To my total surprise and delight, everything appeared normal. As I questioned how this could be, I was told that the lining of the GI tract heals very rapidly, sometimes in less than 24 hours. They even showed me Polaroid photos of my insides. Yep, completely healed.

A devious thought crept into my head. "Do it!", it said. I dismissed it. "Yes, you can," it said again. Hmmmm, I can always stop anytime during the race. Yes! That's it! I'm going to Boston and I will at least, I told myself, start the race!

Armed with a load of iron pills, I arrived at the start of one of the most prestigious races in the world, thrilled at even being there. I ran the race slowly and carefully, monitoring my body signals all the way.

The only real symptom I noticed was that I was cold. Since the temperature was in the low 30's, I didn't think too much about it and just put on the gloves I'd brought and wrapped myself in a plastic garbage bag that some kind, anonymous soul gave me.

My racing singlet read "Hawaii" across the front but, of course, was not visible through the bag. I figured after a few miles when I'd warmed up, I'd take the garbage bag off.

After all, I was pretty proud of being from Hawaii, and I knew that would probably get a lot of attention from the spectators that line the marathon course. I also knew I was going to need the interaction and encouragement from the spectators to help me get through the 26.2 miles I was facing in this apparently weakened condition.

OFF WITH THE GLOVES!

At the 10-mile mark, I took off the gloves. Within minutes, my fingers got so numb I couldn't hold the paper cups supplying liquid refreshment at the aid stations. I knew I needed to drink a lot of water. On went the gloves again.

At the 20-mile mark, I was still cold. This is ridiculous, I thought. But, what the heck, since I was that cold, I figured I had better keep the garbage bag on. In retrospect, I think it was the anemia that kept me from warming up.

Then I saw the official photographer taking pictures of all the runners. Enough's enough, I thought, and off came the garbage bag. I was not about to have my official photo showing me doing the Boston Marathon in a garbage bag!

I finished Boston in decent time and was glad that I'd persisted, gambled and won. What an experience and an exciting race to do!

It took months of iron pills to get me back to normal. First, my hemoglobin came back up to normal over a period of about three months, but it was nearly a year before my iron stores (the serum ferritin test) registered normal.

The main lesson I learned was to monitor the color of my stools. Any bleeding from the GI tract causes darker stools and is immediately obvious when you're a vegetarian. A plant-based diet yields light-colored stools, whereas animal products (digested blood) yields dark stools. I learned that hard races and triathlons may cause several days of GI bleeding. I don't yet know how to prevent this and, consequently, have frequent hemoglobin checks. Reading from medical journals, I know that this is common in long-distance runners.

Most physicians I've talked to seem to think that the bleeding comes from the stomach, but Kent C. Holtzmuller, M.D. claims that the bleeding comes from the colon. He explained that the stomach has a double blood supply and is not as vulnerable to the effects of blood being shifted to the working muscles. But the colon, he claims, has only a single blood supply and, as a result, suffers damage due to the lack of blood to the cells, which then die. He also cited a study done on a group of 35 ultra-marathoners which showed that 85% of them had blood in their stools at the end of the race.

I also found out the hard way that non-steroidal anti-inflammatory medications cause the same thing: GI bleeding. Over the period of several years I've found that there are no anti-inflammatories that will not cause me GI bleeding. As a result I wonder how many of you out there have had GI bleeding and don't know it.

If you're on the typical American, high animal-product diet, you'd have to bleed quite a lot to see black, tarry stools. It's surprising how little physical activity it really does take to cause some bleeding. There is a test for occult bleeding that you might be able to get from your doctor to check at home. I do this test routinely, not just for the GI bleeding from racing, but as a check for colon cancer. This test is recommended annually by The American Cancer Society for patients over 40 or 50 years of age.

CHAPTER FIFTEEN

OSTEOPOROSIS: THE HIDDEN HANDICAP

Sitting here at my newly-found friend, a not-too-user-friendly computer, I am building stronger bones. I am sipping blackstrap molasses, a spoonful in a cup of hot water. One tablespoon of this delicious coffee substitute provides our bodies with not only 131 mg of calcium, but also a wonderful bonus of 3.2 mg of iron.

Contrast this with the negative effects of coffee. A 1990 study of 38,564 men and women showed that heavy coffee drinking increased the risk of dying of heart disease, even after allowing for other important risk factors such as heavy smoking and high blood pressure.

Coffee also robs calcium from the bones, contains a central nervous system stimulant with its depressing aftereffects, and is suspected of being a possible carcinogen. Heavy coffee drinkers also had higher levels of cholesterol than those who drank more moderate amounts.

One cannot escape the flood of advertisements extolling the virtues of calcium. Yes, of course, calcium is important, but why is it that the strongest bones are found in the people of the world who have supposedly the "worst" diets? And why is it that the people who eat the most dairy products have the highest incidence of osteoporosis?

And how did it get ordained that cattle were to be the suppliers of our calcium? Why not horses, or dogs, or whales?

When you stop to think about the purpose of a species' milk-producing glands, it is to supply its own newborn with a uniquely-formulated sustenance until it can get food on its own. Each species has a different amount of protein, depending on how fast the infants grow. No other species drinks the breast secretions of another species!

Although the returns are not all in yet, it appears that our Western high protein diet is a major culprit in draining calcium out of our bones. This coupled with a sedentary lifestyle predisposes us to a condition of weakened, fragile bones.

It is frequently said that someone fell and broke their hip, when in fact, their hip broke and then they fell. Or that someone just sneezed and broke a rib. There's something drastically wrong here, since it seems logical to assume that our bones are supposed to last a lifetime.

There are studies that show that vegetarian women have stronger bones than meat-eating women. Tennis players have much more dense bones (by 16%) in their tennis-playing arms versus their non-playing arms. Both tennis players and swimmers had greater bone density than their non-exercising control counterparts.

These three studies alone are convincing evidence that both diet and exercise are important in growing and maintaining strong, dense bones.

It is frequently said that genetics plays a role in the incidence of osteoporosis. Well, it does to the extent that we are predisposed to the effects of too much protein in our diets or too little exercise. There are other studies, however, that show that when people from Africa (with strong, dense bones) migrate to the U.S. and consume the typical Western-type diet, they start showing the effects of osteoporosis.

Then there's the myth that pregnant and lactating women need to drink milk in order to grow strong, healthy babies and then be able to provide them enough breast milk after their birth. Since three-quarters of the world's population has never consumed dairy products, it seems ridiculous that the medical profession as a whole still so actively promotes the consumption of dairy products.

In addition, there is a great deal of evidence that cow's milk causes so many problems such as a high incidence of allergies, middle ear infections, food sensitivities, constipation, and too much protein in the child's diet.

So, what's the role of osteoporosis in something like an Ironman Triathlon? Can you think of a better way to build strong bones than to exercise in three sports? Swimming and biking, in spite of being low (or no) impact sports, still require that muscles pull on bones. These forces are enough to keep bones strong and counteract the effects that tend to tear bone down.

There is a principle that students of anatomy and physiology learn called "Wolff's Law." This says, in effect, that bones grow as strong as they need to be. This means that bones are active, alive, and constantly remodeling themselves. Osteoclasts are cells that tear down bone, and osteoblasts are cells that build up bone. These processes cause a continuous exchange of bony material in response to the demands that we place on them.

Even more effective in building bone mass, however, is running, although its effects seem to be limited primarily to lower body and spine. Since the most serious fractures from osteoporosis are in the hips and spine, running should be the most efficient exercise to counter the effects of osteoporosis, or preferably, to build strong bones and prevent the disease from ever occurring.

A little aside here: Running also promotes healthy disks, the little gelatinous cushions between each of the vertebra in the spine. You've probably heard frequently about "slipped" or "ruptured" disks. For years it was thought that this was what caused so many back problems. In actuality, it was usually weakness of the muscles whose job it is to support the spine. Running helps strengthen these muscles.

It was recently discovered that running also causes a "loading" of the body's weight on the disks as the body impacts the ground. As it springs off the ground for the next stride, there is an "un-loading." The effect of these loading forces is the "pumping" in of nutrients and oxygen and the removal of metabolic wastes and carbon dioxide out. As a result, most runners have strong disks and back muscles.

There are definite hormonal influences on bone modeling and remodeling plus the positive effects of Vitamin D. Since most of us can do little about our hormone status and don't care to get more sun exposure than is necessary or convenient, diet and exercise are the two most viable options to develop and keep strong bones.

Another interesting aspect of how marvelously these human bodies are put together has to do with the intestinal tract taking what it needs from the food as it passes through. For example, it is known that when the body is anemic, more iron is absorbed from the food passing through the intestinal tract. This is measured by a test called the TIBC, (the Total Iron-Binding Capacity). When we need more iron, we absorb more.

The same is true of calcium. There is, however, no neat little test like the TIBC to tell us how much we are absorbing. This explains why women in Africa who get only 200-400 mg of calcium a day have strong, dense bones after twenty years of multiple pregnancies and long lactation periods.

CALCIUM PILL DEFICIENCY?

For all the reasons noted above, we don't need calcium pills to build strong bones. Additionally, studies have shown that giving calcium pills to people who already have osteoporosis does no good. Actually, even adults who gorged on high-calcium foods did not lose less bone than those with a low calcium intake, according to a 1990 University of Michigan study.

Post-menopausal women can be given estrogen to try to enhance their bone-building capabilities, but not all women want to or can take estrogen. I'm a good case in point. Because my type of cancer is estrogen receptor positive, this means that taking estrogen would be like adding gasoline to the cancerous fires.

As a precaution I do have annual bone density measurements, and apparently, my regime is working. Although I have had some bone loss, I'm still at the top of the charts as far as bone density for women my age. The reason I call it the "hidden handicap," is that so many women from the age of 35 on are going around with bones that are losing a significant amount of calcium. They have no idea that they are heading for fractures, height shrinkage, rib cages resting on hip bones, and dowager's humps.

In my case I've had a number of stress fractures, nine to be exact. Skeptics could say that my system is not working, and I have to admit that I questioned my regime at first. After much research, however, the concensus seems to be that I was overtraining. In my eagerness to improve coupled with my love of running, I was racing the week after doing as stressful an event as the Ironman.

No wonder I was having stress fractures, many medics said. I was not getting nearly enough recovery time! In fact, a general rule of thumb is to take one easy training day for every mile of strenuous racing. I've never been able to even come close to that! Ever since I've backed off on hard runs soon after hard races, no more stress fractures.

In order to insure that I do get adequate calcium, however, I do try to eat some calcium-rich foods daily. In addition to the blackstrap molasses trick, I also eat a lot of green leafy vegetables. In fact, if a day goes by that I haven't had a large serving of broccoli, I'll have it the last thing at night!

HIGH PROTEIN CAN MEAN WEAK BONES!

One of the other dietary factors in osteoporosis relates to America's long-standing love affair with protein.

For years now, foods have been marketed as being "High Protein" because it helped sell. There are high protein pills, high protein powders, high protein cosmetics, high protein anything and everything!

So, what happens when you eat too much protein? You go into negative calcium balance as the body tries to compensate for the excess amino acids. It draws calcium, (which is a base needed to offset the increased acid), out of the blood. To replenish the supply in the blood, the body in turn draws it out of the bones. An occasional excess is not critical, but when people eat high protein meals twenty-one times a week, the effect is cumulative.

An example is the Eskimo who, with their high protein (fish) diets, have an extremely high incidence of osteoporosis at a very early age. Women in their TWENTIES have been diagnosed with osteoporosis.

Men, too, are not immune from the effects of osteoporosis. Although it usually starts later in life for them, it can still be a very crippling disease. It can cause falls, leaving a person with a fractured pelvis and totally bedridden. Once a person is bedridden, they have NO weight-bearing on their bones which, in turn, rapidly accelerates bone loss.

These losses are not insignificant! When astronauts return from outer space trips, they have measurable bone loss. Fortunately, young people have the hormones to help reverse the damage and lay down new bone. Older people, women past menopause in particular, do not have enough hormones to reverse the bone loss. The damage may be permanent!

Take heed and know that your bones are another good reason to get a lot of exercise and eat right!

Fig. 15.1 Completing a half-marathon 3 days after diagnosis of two tibial stress fractures. *PictureMan*

CHAPTER SIXTEEN

ARTHRITIS: DIET <u>DOES</u> MAKE A DIFFERENCE

One of the presumptions made in earlier chapters is that this body of mine is fairly average and that it responds to good and bad things done to it just as your body would. While I recognize that there are individual differences, there is much more that is similar among us humans.

We could not otherwise all have the same blood tests done and show "normal" ranges, and surgeons would be surprised each time they opened each one of us up. And we know that this is not usually the case. We are all very predictable.

We all are aware that arthritis is a fairly common malady. We hear pronouncements from the Arthritis Foundation; we read articles in newspapers and magazines about arthritis; and most of us know people who are afflicted with this painful joint disease.

What we are told is that it's a rather common affliction; that it's an expected part of growing old (at least in the degenerative osteoarthritis form); that there's no cure; and that diet does not affect arthritis one way or the other.

One day about thirteen years ago (that would have made me 42 years old), I went to see a doctor because of the gradual onset of a stiff, painful back. Waking up in the morning, I could hardly bend over. I had to use both hands hanging on to the wall to lower myself down to the toilet, and it took about 10 minutes of gradual movement to loosen my back enough to put my shoes on.

X-rays were taken and a hands-on examination was performed. The verdict was osteoarthritis. Nothing serious, I was told. Just a part of growing older. My running, they said, was probably aggravating it and I should just resign myself to what was said to be inevitable.

No, they said, there was nothing I could do to help it. But there was this new medication, a non-steroidal anti-inflammatory, naproxen, which should ease the discomfort. It is not a cure, I was told, and only treated the symptoms. I was probably going to have to take it the rest of my life.

THE MIRACLES OF MODERN MEDICINE!

The pills were great! I woke up each morning able to move without pain, totally flexible, and thought wonderful things about the miracles of modern medicine.

During the ensuing years, I'd periodically be asked by doctors if I was on any medication. I'd usually say none. This routine became such a "normal" part of my life that it was just like taking vitamin pills.

Then came the medical emergency described previously in the chapter on anemia. The doctors at the Emergency Room at Tripler asked me the standard question and I gave the standard answer, no medications.

It was only after that diagnosis of anemia that I called my "diet" doctor, John McDougall, to ask him if he was sure that I was getting enough iron on my vegetarian diet. After all, I'd read that red meat gave you "heme iron", the "best" source of iron. He reassured me, saying that if I was suffering from iron-deficiency anemia, that I could be sure that I was losing blood somewhere. His guess was that I was having GI bleeding. I told him that I did have it periodically from hard or long races. He then said, "Are you taking any medication?" I started my automatic reply.

"Whoa, yes! I completely forgot about naproxen. I've been taking that for years now."

He said, "That's probably what's doing it!"

I immediately stopped the pills, expecting to return to the painful, stiff back of the pre-naproxen days. To my surprise and delight, there was not even a hint of pain or stiffness.

When I discussed this with Dr. McDougall, he was not the least surprised. He stated, "Despite what the Arthritis Foundation claims, diet DOES make a difference!"

Apparently, when I made the dietary changes due to the cancer, I inadvertently did the best thing possible for my arthritis. A recent study showed that the common nonsteroidal, anti-inflammatory drugs, like the one prescribed for me, work by inhibiting the hormones called prostaglandins. This process can actually cause the opposite effect! It can destroy more joint tissue than the arthritis itself.

Another interesting fact is that the incidence of arthritis follows the same pattern described earlier with regard to all the common diet-related cancers. Inflammatory arthritis is most common in those countries that eat a high-fat diet, and is rare in those countries on a low-fat diet. And, again, it's not heredity because when those people migrate to the U.S. and adopt our high-fat diet, they soon get arthritis at the same frequency as the people around them.

The theory as to why this happens has to do with the reaction of the animal proteins in our bodies. As these foreign proteins enter our bloodstream, our body's immune system forms antibodies against them, as they would with any foreign protein. In people prone to arthritis, these "immune complexes" are filtered out of the bloodstream and end up in the joints. Here they act like tiny slivers of wood, causing the pain, swelling, and inflammation of the joints.

In the ensuing years I have had no arthritic symptoms in my back or anywhere else. And this after a medical prediction that I would be on arthritis medication for the "rest of my life!"

I also believe that the strenuous exercise program I'm on helps. When the muscles supporting both sides of a joint are weak, they let too much stress on the joint surfaces. And, conversely, when muscles are very strong, they support the joint structures and protect them from unnatural wear and tear.

Just my own theory, but it seems to be working. I recall in Kenneth Cooper's book, "Aerobics", he talked about the importance of having strong abdominal and back muscles to support the spinal column. Running will do that and has been responsible for the elimination of the back aches that I had for the years before starting a running program.

Of course, there are other exercises that strengthen the back and other joints. Just find one that you enjoy, eliminate all animal products from your diet, and you may cure all your joint aches and pains!

CHAPTER SEVENTEEN
THE CRASH I CAN'T REMEMBER:
SAFETY COMES FIRST

As if all the other medical problems I'd been having to contend with weren't enough, I had a bike crash that laid me up for six weeks. Since it happened seven weeks before my first Ironman, things looked pretty grim for my getting to the start line.

Preparation for any race involves knowing the course. Since the Ironman bike course was on the Big Island of Hawaii, and since my father and step-mother, Les and Jean Nunes, lived in Kona, I had a wonderful opportunity to visit them and check out the entire bike course.

My father has always had all sorts of misgivings about my riding a bike on these roads in Hawaii, feeling that they are fraught with danger. And it wasn't as if I felt otherwise; it was that I was willing to take the risk. Although by no means an expert cyclist, I did feel that I took no unreasonable risks.

So it was in late August, 1984 that I was tooling along the Queen Kaahumanu Highway at about mile 97 of the 112-mile course. I was just a few miles from the village of Kona. The last thing I remember is passing the turn-off to the airport, thinking how good I felt and confident that I was going to be able to do the bike leg with no problems.

The next thing I remembered, it was 10:30 p.m. and I was in a hospital bed, feeling pain literally from head to toe.

I asked the nurse what happened and where was my bike. She laughed and said, "We told you; don't you remember?"

Then a medical technologist came in to draw some blood and started talking to me like she knew me. I was totally confused! The med tech laughed and said, "You've asked me at least a dozen times already, 'what happened and where is my bike?'"

I said incredulously, "I asked YOU?"

"Yeah," she said, "when I drew your blood this afternoon." "You asked everybody in sight."

"But, hospital personnel wouldn't know things like where my bike was..."

"Well, you asked them anyway. Then when they told you, two minutes later, you asked them again, and again!"

Boy, was my mind reeling from the shock. Here I was, in a hospital, not knowing how I got there, and people are telling me things that I didn't even remember saying. Slowly, I was able to piece the story together.

A passing pick-up truck had apparently grazed me and knocked me off my bike. I was found unconscious by the side of the road. A motorist who witnessed the crash called an ambulance with his CB radio. The ambulance crew checked vital signs and determined that I had suffered a concussion, that I was not in need of an IV, that I had suffered some kind of impact fall, and that I was going to require the services of an emergency room.

THANK GOODNESS FOR HELMETS!

Luckily, I had a helmet on. No, I shouldn't say "luckily." I learned from my very first days of cycling that a helmet was an absolute necessity while riding and, therefore, wouldn't even go around the block without one.

In any case, I hit the ground hard enough to crack the helmet open and sustain a three-inch long cut on the side of my head. My feet had been tightly strapped to the pedals by metal toe clips. The metal straps had been sheared off.

Now in a hospital bed, I tried to move. The stabbing pain in my hip brought me up short. "Oh, my God, what happened to me," I wailed, on the verge of tears. They tried to reassure me that I was going to be all right, and I said, "I've got an Ironman in seven weeks!" They shook their heads, saying "No way!"

The doctor shook his head, too. "No way!"

"Look, just forget it for this year, get well, and plan for it next year."

But I had my own thoughts about what I was going to do. I'd invested too much in this venture, thinking that if the breast cancer couldn't stop me, I wasn't about to let anything else keep me from doing it.

I wanted out of that bed and to get back to my training routine. I felt just like I did after my mastectomies. The plotting and scheming started immediately, primarily because I didn't want my conditioning to go down the tubes! All I could think about was "Let me out of here!" I wanted to get back to my running, swimming, and, yes, biking!

More than anything else, what bothered me was the amnesia. I could remember passing the airport road, but they found me two miles past it. I couldn't remember being hit, all the people that stopped to help me, the ambulance ride, the emergency room repairs consisting of stitching up the gash in my head, the X-rays, the blood-drawing, all the bandages covering what they said was a "seven-point landing," and who knows what else. And the fact that my brain seemed to be doing a short circuit number: "what happened? where's my bike?"

The nurses thought it was rather amusing, but I was really upset. Why couldn't I remember?

The doctor on call at the time was Frank Ferren, M.D., who was himself an Ironman and who had, as it turned out, treated a number of bike crash victims. He explained that what I had was anterograde and retrograde amnesia; that is, after a concussion, people sometimes forgot things that happened immediately PRIOR to the impact as well as after.

As I was in the hospital for almost a week, I spent hours mentally digging through my brain cells. "Remember, damn you, remember!" It was months later that I was still mentally digging and all of a sudden remembered sharp, needle-like pains. That was the stitching up the cut in my head!

Then I recalled a vague image of an elevator. Yes, that was a ride on a gurney up to my hospital room. Then I remembered three or four people trying to move me off the gurney. I obviously had not been sedated; I had screamed in pain as they lifted me up onto the bed.

The hip pain was no better a week later. When I went to see an orthopedic specialist back in Honolulu, the doctor ordered a bone scan. This test, which involves injecting a radioactive substance into the blood that, over the period of a couple of hours, settles into areas of bone injury, disclosed a hip fracture.

Not only was my first Ironman at risk, but I'd entered the Waikiki Roughwater Swim which was to take place that weekend. This was important to me because it represented the first event of the Ironman. If I couldn't do this event, I really was in trouble. I had never really given up the idea that I was going to be there for the start of the Ironman, no matter what!

The orthopedic specialist had the bone scan on the lighted screen. Shaking his head, he said, "No, there's definitely a fracture there. It's going to be six to eight weeks on crutches. Forget the Ironman."

Almost in desperation, I said, "What about swimming? Swimming should be good for it, shouldn't it?"

Looking at me as if I'd lost my marbles, he almost pleaded, "Look, let those bones knit! If you keep moving them, you're taking a chance on permanent damage to your hip. There's a risk of necrosis! Necrosis, death of the bone!"

Now I really was in trouble. How could I tell him I'd been swimming daily since getting out of the hospital. He didn't look like he'd understand if I told him how careful I was about keeping the hip immobile and that I was not kicking my feet and legs at all.

Thoroughly frightened and chastened, I gave up. They're right; forget it.

That lasted until I got home. I guess the fear wore off, and I found myself scheming and trying to decide how to at least **start** the Roughwater Swim. Because there were course marshalls on surf boards all along the 2.4 mile course, I could drop out at any time.

All that was left to do was get somebody to take the crutches from me after I got in the water, and get them down to the finish line 2.4 miles away, wade into the water with them so I could walk up the beach to the swim finish line. People thought I was crazy to even think of it but finally agreed when they saw I was determined to swim in that race with or without their help.

YOU CAN DO ANYTHING YOU WANT TO DO!

And, so it was, in 1984, that I learned that swimming for a triathlete is primarily an upper body sport. I found that my time was not that much slower, that dragging legs still acted as a rudder, and that I could do things that I "shouldn't" if I wanted to badly enough.

Now, this is not to say that the doctors were wrong. The safest course, surely, is to rest after an injury. It's just that you're taking a chance if you persist in training in the face of an injury. I was really lucky, and, in fact, I healed much faster than the medical estimates indicated I would. I was off the crutches in four weeks instead of the 6-8 weeks predicted. Based on the experience of a whole lot of injuries and seven surgeries, I have seen that the fit athlete heals much faster than the average, sedentary person.

Fig. 17.1 Coming up on the finish line of the Waikiki Roughwater Swim 2 weeks after pelvic fracture. PictureMan

The rest of the recovery proceeded at an accelerated pace. After the Roughwater Swim, I started toying with the idea of getting on a stationary bicycle. I argued with myself for another week, and thought, what the heck, if it hurts, I'll just stop.

And sure enough, after just a couple of minutes, it did. I did not persist. I wasn't really disappointed or depressed either, though, thinking that I'd just keep trying until the day that it was okay. And I'd know exactly when that day was.

The next morning I was thinking that I'd had another 24 hours of healing time. Time to try again! And, to my surprise, I could go four minutes before pain set in.

And the third day, the time doubled again! I got very excited as I computed the recovery rate. Now, I already knew I had the swim handled; here it looked as though the bike was going to be okay, too.

Sure enough, each day I saw this tremendous rate of improvement. Ironically, I was also entered in the Honolulu Advertiser Century Ride which came at about the fifth week after the accident. Here was my chance to see if I could do a 100-miler on the bike.

To my greatest surprise and delight, I made it through the entire 100 miles without too much pain. I knew it then! I was going to do at least the first two parts of the Ironman for sure!

On the medical check-up scheduled five weeks after the crash, I told the doctor that I thought I was really healing ahead of schedule. He poked, prodded, and apparently was satisfied that I was not going to yell out in pain.

He backed off, putting his hands on his hips and said, "Let's see if you can walk." After one week in the hospital and four weeks on crutches, I almost panicked.

"Walk?"

I suddenly got cold feet. I'd grown attached to those crutches and was not sure that I was really ready for the real show-down. What if I **couldn't** walk? The Ironman was now only two weeks away.

I slowly, carefully put some weight on my right foot. It seemed okay. A little more weight. Still okay. The doctor put out a steadying hand, and I put the rest of the weight on my foot.

"OHMYGOD!," I whooped! I'm standing and nothing hurt! Another slow series of weight transfers, this time to the left foot. And, ohmygod, no pain! Another step, and another. I let the joy sink in, "I'm OK...I'M OK!"

The doctor said, "OK, now just take it easy. You've still got a ways to go. Don't get exuberant and do too much."

RUNNING TO RECOVERY!

The next day I ran for two minutes and was about to discover that getting back to running was just like getting back to biking. Except that the Ironman was now only 13 days away and I was going to have to run a full marathon.

I couldn't keep doubling my time, so I stopped a week before the race with a single 12-mile run. At that point I didn't care what happened, because however it worked out, I would be there at the start line and would go as far as I could.

As it turned out, I had a wonderful first Ironman. Because of all that had occurred the previous seven weeks, survival was all that was on my mind. There was not even the slightest wish to "race." That, as it turned out, was the best thing that could have happened to me. It forced me to pace myself and, as a result, I completed the entire event in 14 hours 49 minutes.

The official results weren't available until the next morning. When I saw that I was one MINUTE from placing in my age group, I was so excited that I immediately started plotting my training schedule. Just think what I could do if I could **train** for the last seven weeks, I mused. Just wait til next year! On top of that, I was going to be in a new age group, the 50-54 year olds. It would help being the youngest in my group instead of what I had been, the oldest.

Now, if I could only remember that ambulance ride!

CHAPTER EIGHTEEN

RECONSTRUCTING A BODY AND A LIFE

Amid those harrowing days of dealing with the diagnosis of cancer and getting ready for the mastectomy, there appeared a small ray of sunshine. I'd remembered reading about reconstructive surgery and asked my surgeon about it. He said he'd arrange to have a consultation with the Plastic Surgery Department.

One of the books I'd read said that there was a "quaint" theory that still existed in the minds of some plastic surgeons regarding breast reconstruction. They were recommending that breast reconstruction be withheld from women for approximately two years.

It was felt that if a woman had to do without for at least that period of time, when the reconstruction was accomplished, she'd be totally grateful for whatever she got. It seems that the technology was not that great, and, in fact, some of the least successful results bordered on the grotesque!

I had expected to see the plastic surgeon before my mastectomy, but he was "too busy." This dismayed me because another book had suggested that the plastic surgeon participate in the mastectomy surgical procedure itself so as to ensure that nothing was done to complicate the later surgery.

I had no choice then but to take my chances. As it turned out, there was a good reason for the plastic surgeon to be there.

When I finally got in to see the plastic surgeon about two months later, he looked at the location of the two drain tube scars that had been put almost in the middle of where a new breast would be constructed. He shook his head and said that it was too bad they were placed there; the resultant scar tissue just made his job a little harder! I saw nothing to gain by protesting and just heaved a big sigh.

There was, however, a change in the surgical procedure between the first and second mastectomies. The second surgical procedure had the drain tubes toward my back, completely away from the reconstructive site. I felt gratified, at least, to see some progress being made but wondered how many other women, their surgeons, and plastic surgeons had yet to go through this same learning curve.

Actually, today in some cases, they will even do a simultaneous mastectomy and reconstruction. I've visited a couple of these patients and was amazed that they had no idea how lucky they were. One patient thought that every breast cancer patient was treated that way!

At the time of my first visit to the plastic surgeon, he examined me and said that I was an excellent candidate for reconstruction. I was elated and asked how soon.

The answer was, "As soon as the scar softens, and the skin stretches enough to take the implant." In an effort to get any possible vagrant cancer cells lying under the skin and in the subcutaneous fat, surgeons cut away as much skin as possible and scrape the subcutaneous fat from the "flaps" they create to cover the now-bare chest and close the wound.

The resulting upper torso now looks flatter than a prepubertal child's. The ribs stand out, and it's difficult to move the arms in any direction due to the skin having been stretched tightly to cover the chest wall.

The plastic surgeon said that this scar-softening and skin-stretching process would take a minimum of from six months to a year, and in some cases, never. This is when they do skin grafts, a prospect I did not relish at all. I very conscientiously did my stretching exercises and even pulled on the skin for good measure.

It must have worked because during my third visit at four months, he said, "We're getting there!"

We planned my surgery for two months later.

Looking back, I don't know how I got through those days. Every shower, every swim, every glance in the mirror was a stark reminder of not only a breastless form but also of the cancer.

Stuffing bras just did not do the trick. Every time I raised my arm, the whole bra slid up. When I lowered my arm, the bra and prosthesis stayed up! What an uncomfortable, miserable way to live. I felt like I was holding my breath until the day of the surgery.

The day I was admitted to the hospital, I had to go through all the usual pre-op tests. This time, in contrast to the previous times, I did so with great joy and cheer. I grinned at the lab techs as they drew my blood. I babbled on as the EKG (electrocardiogram to check the condition of my heart) was taken, stating that this was the last time that electrodes were going to be placed on this chicken-breasted form.

The plastic surgeon came next with his purple marker and drew all sorts of marks on me. A nipple line across the chest so that the nipples would be even, two circles for the areolas (the pigmented areas around the nipples), two lower lines for the inframammary fold (medical talk for the lower curves of my new breasts), and marks on my ears and thighs.

My ear lobes were going to contribute a wedge of skin which was to be sculpted into two nipples, and my upper inner thighs were to contribute the skin for two new areolas.

"Just the right hint of pink, too," the plastic surgeon joked!

That night in the hospital I could hardly sleep. The plastic surgeon had impressed on me that the choices I had made as to the exact size and location of my new breasts were irreversible. I'd better be sure, he said.

I got up several times during the night to check myself in the mirror. Were they going to be too big? Too small? Too high? Too low? Too far apart? Too close together?

My God, what did they used to look like? I couldn't remember! I thought then that maybe some of those surgeons had the right idea; make then wait and they'll be grateful for anything!

And I was, for a while. The healing seemed to go very well for the first month, but one day I noticed that one "breast" was a little high. Or was it that the other one was too low? Over the period of a couple of months, one or the other was happening. I returned for a check-up and remarked on the discrepancy.

DON'T I GET A MATCHED SET?

The plastic surgeon brushed off my concern, saying that nothing on our bodies that is paired is identical, that our feet are of two different sizes, leg lengths, etc. I said that I agreed to a point, but this had passed that point!

I felt like I was a ship whose cargo had shifted, that I was "listing" to one side. Finally, when he realized that I was not going to be mollified, he agreed to do the correction.

By this time I was an old hand at surgery, and the thought of another operation didn't bother me in the least. It was a process, much like a marathon. You've got to go through a lot of discomfort, sometimes, to get what you want, and, like a marathon, it's worth it in the end!

Today, the whole process has been somewhat reversed. My new breasts are so much a part of me and my body image that I've forgotten what I used to look like. And the best news of all is that as I grow older, they will never sag.

I sometimes chuckle to myself as I conjure up the image of a 90-year-old triathlete with these two nice, high, firm, round bosoms!

CHAPTER NINETEEN

IRONMEN CAN BE BEAUTIFUL:

BEAUTY TIPS FOR ATHLETES

One of the more common misconceptions is that female athletes are "jocks" or "jockettes." With that is the implication that being athletic is the antithesis to being feminine — that a "beautiful competitor" is an oxymoron.

As I got more and more into hard training and competition, I felt the inevitable conflicts occurring. If I do a swim workout, I'll ruin my hair and, well, forget about make-up.

The same is true of biking and running. Putting a bicycle helmet on my head meant a flattened, sweaty head of hair. And who can present a decent face when you're dripping with perspiration.

Another conflict: On race day one usually has to get up way before the crack of dawn — sometimes 3:00 or 4:00 in the morning. Who could possibly be thinking of looking gorgeous at a time like that, especially when one's mind needs to be on race preparation.

Not being willing to give up all vestiges of attractiveness, I developed a bunch of beauty tricks. Some of them are very practical and some purely frivolous. I would not give up any of them. See if any of these suit you.

1. **Permanent eye liner and brows.** When applied correctly, this make-up technique is done once and forgotten forever. You wake up with beautiful eyes and brows; you come out of the water with beautiful eyes and brows; you cross the finish line with beautiful eyes and brows. I've had mine long enough that I "own" them,

feeling they are so much a part of me that I forget that I ever really needed them.

In fact, with the liner and brows, I get by without any other make-up. This really paid off when the reporters from the New Zealand Herald took photos of me right after crossing the finish line of that Ironman. The picture on the front page of that newspaper shows eyes that could have just stepped out of a make-up artist's studio! (Well, almost!)

2. Disposable extended wear contact lenses.

When I reached the age of 47, I finally had to face the fact that reading small print was becoming impossible. As I'd looked around at others approaching 40, they were having to convert to bifocal glasses. I thought that maybe I'd escape that fate, but, no, I was just lucky in being able to put it off longer.

When I mentioned to my boss that I was going to have to see an eye doctor, he revealed to me his "secret." He wore contact lenses with one eye set for close-up reading and the other for distance.

Since my distance vision was fine, I asked Stan Yamane, my new optometric doctor, if I could wear just one lens. He said he didn't see any reason why not. I asked if he had any other patients doing that, and he said that I would be the first.

Well, that was a **little** scary but I figured I didn't have much to lose. And it worked like a charm.

For nearly ten years now, I have been able to avoid eye glasses and it's been wonderful. I come out of the water being able to see everything. If I have a bike problem, I can see close-up details. And after the race, I can read the race results, and since I am a reporter for Triathlon Today, I can start writing the story without having to find eye glasses.

When the disposable lenses became available, I was first in line to try them. They have been wonderful for the six months that I've been using them. And, besides, Dr. Yamane figures that I save the equivalent of two workweeks a year in time by not having to insert, remove, clean, sterilize, etc. my lenses. The freedom is wonderful!

3. **"Permanent" jewelry.** My Aunt Dorisse taught me when I was young that it was better to have good jewelry, i.e., the "real" thing. Even if this meant fewer pieces, they should be tasteful and, if need be, expensive. After I lost my ear lobes to the plastic surgeon who made them into nipples, I decided that I was going to treat myself to a pair of large, diamond stud earrings.

Now, who wants to keep a treasure like that in a safe deposit box or in a vault. I decided that I wanted to wear mine—all the time. So as not to chance losing them in the ocean or anywhere else, I bent the posts and put the backs on as usual. Now, they CAN'T come off. Well, I can take them off to clean them, but I don't think I will ever lose them accidentally.

I also wear a 24-carat gold bracelet with a clasp that can't come undone. A good jeweler can solder the fastenings, ensuring that they won't be lost. The reason I emphasize "tasteful" is that you will wear them on ALL occasions. And I, for one, can't think of an occasion when diamond earrings and gold bracelets are not nice to have on.

Rings, however, are a problem. I've not found a way to prevent losing them and have just quit wearing them. I do have some gold chains that I wear around my neck. If you have the clasps checked at least annually, there is a good chance you will never lose them. Again, I'd rather use them, taking a chance on losing them, than have them sit in a safe deposit box where no one can enjoy them. And, as with the eye liner and brows, it's nice to come out of the water or cross the finish line looking feminine and as glamorous as I can.

4. **Hair.** I've had it short; I've had it down to my waist. Either way works for me, but short is certainly a lot easier to stuff under a swim cap, helmet, or shampoo after the multitudinous workouts we have to undergo.

The only procedure I really need is a permanent wave, which I do myself. It's so easy and you really save a bundle. There is probably only one prerequisite, and that is have a simple hair style. And when you exude good health, you don't need to rely on fancy hair-do's to make you beautiful. Then when you cross the finish line of a race, all you have to do is run a comb through your hair. You'll look perfectly groomed, ready for the cameras!

5. **Skin.** What applies to hair also applies to skin. When your blood is healthy, laden with nutrients, and your circulation top-notch, your skin fairly glows. You don't need any kind of cover-up other than a sun block. Sweat, salt water, chlorine, etc. will not harm your skin. But the SUN WILL!

There is no quicker way to age your skin than with exposure to the sun. Since it's a little difficult to get in your training in the dark, the only solution is to use as close to a total sun block as possible. There are some on the market, like Beaver, with a sun protection factor (SPF) of 43, which means that, theoretically, you could spend 43 hours in the sun and get the exposure of one hour.

If you're allergic to one of the common ingredients in sun block, PABA, get one with PABA esters which should eliminate the allergic reactions. The application of a sun block should be an automatic morning ritual, even if you don't plan on a sun work-out. It'll pay off as you get older!

6. **Sun glasses.** The sun's damage is not limited to only your skin. It will also damage your eyes, causing cataracts to form. Studies have shown that blue-eyed people in the tropics who do not wear sun glasses have a much greater prevalence of cataracts than brown-eyed

people who wear sun glasses. Just make sure the lenses are coated with a filter to screen out the UV (ultraviolet) rays.

Sun glasses also tend to minimize the frown lines between the eyes and squinting (laughingly called laugh lines), both of which also lead to wrinkling of the face.

7. **Legs.** I'm sure you've seen women, some even quite young, who have disfiguring spider veins or even large, knotty varicose veins in their legs. These are preventable but probably not reversible. To prevent them, you need to eat a high-fiber diet like the one described in the diet chapter and get lots of large muscle exercise like running and biking.

Varicose veins are caused by failure of the venous valves to stop the backflow of blood as it journeys from the feet up to the heart. As you can imagine, there's a lot of pressure from that blood trying to go upstream, and incompetent valves will let the blood pool in the veins. That pooling leads to tortuous, twisted, knotted veins. Not only is it unattractive, but it can be dangerous as blood clots can form in the stagnating blood. It has been said that exercise is the body's second heart.

A lot of people feel that varicose veins are hereditary because they run in families. Well, naturally, the tendency to have the same kind of valves your parents do is inherited. There is nothing, however, you can do about your heredity at this late date, but there is something you can do to improve the health of your veins: Exercise!

Oh, yes, are you wondering what on earth a high-fiber diet has to do with varicose veins? People on low-fiber diets have bowel problems like constipation. Constipation causes straining which puts tremendous pressures on the veins in the lower half of the body. So not only will they get varicose veins in their legs, they'll also get hemorrhoids!

8. **Feet.** With proper-fitting shoes, or preferably, no shoes (nature's way, after all), we should all have beautiful

feet. Unfortunately, it doesn't turn out that way. Athletes have black toe nails from running downhill in too-short shoes; blisters from rubbing on areas where there is friction; thickened toenails from hitting against the ends of shoes with a too-small toe box. These are usually temporary conditions which are relieved by getting rid of the offending shoes.

Feet expand with usage and most people find their feet start growing a size or two when they take up running. So be sure to get a size large enough to accommodate the spreading foundation for your body.

Feet also tend to expand from morning to evening, so buy shoes late in the day. Bike shoes, on the other hand, are fitted differently. They need to be very snug as the body's forces are transmitted through them to the bike pedal. And you will probably need to do little, if any, walking in them.

Since most people tend to develop callouses on the bottoms of their feet, take every opportunity you can to walk barefoot in the sand. Not only will this strengthen foot muscles, it will grind off the callouses, leaving baby-smooth skin!

Personally, I think most of the advice given in the so-called "beauty books" is a bunch of garbage, intending only to cater to the dreams of people who want to be more attractive. After all, we know now that the high-protein and liquid protein diets of the past ruin our kidneys and bones. Any low calorie diet just puts the body into a starvation mode and causes it to add more fat when the deprivation period is over, which, of course, is inevitable.

We also know that exercise is the only way to keep a beautiful body and a sexy silhouette throughout your life span. Muscles that don't get used will atrophy and become weak and slack. Sexy curves are from toned muscles, not from silicone or a scalpel. Bones that don't get stressed regularly also suffer the same fate of atrophy and weakness.

All I'm offering here is a way to make lifetime exercise a lot of fun, a very strong habit, and a major commitment. I know that once you try this lifestyle, you'll never go back to the old way — ever!

You don't need make-up to make your skin glow. Your "rouge" is the natural color of the vasomotor flush of strenuous exercise. Your "foundation" is the soft, dewy, fine-pored skin which is the result of good nutrients brought to the epithelial cells by a strong circulatory system. Lipstick is unnecessary when lips are healthy and pink from the underlying bright red blood.

Teeth look whiter when gums are pinker. And don't forget to floss daily, because all the exercise in the world does not get rid of the plaque that develops around the gum lines, which can cause the loss of even healthy teeth.

Bright, sexy eyes are the result of an adequate amount of the deep sleep of the physically exhausted plus the enthusiasm for life and the joy of living one feels when the body is treated as it would be if we only came with an "owner's manual."

So, forget about artificial beauty tricks. When in doubt about whether or not to try something, use as your guidance, is it natural? Now, that doesn't automatically mean if it isn't, don't do it. It just means you have to know what you are doing and evaluate the risk versus the benefit.

Just know that when you are your healthiest, you will automatically be at your most beautiful — for the rest of your life!

CHAPTER TWENTY
IRONMAN: KONA, HAWAII

The tiny Kona village on the Big Island of Hawaii gets transformed every October as the Ironman competitors start arriving.

The air is absolutely electric with the tension and deadly seriousness of so many of the triathletes. Alii Drive connects the swim start and finish, the bike start with the bike finish and run start, and for the finale, the finish for the marathon.

For the six miles in between, there are throngs of people and cars parked along the roadside offering their local, homemade version of support and whatever kind of aid is necessary and legal. But that's where all the help ends.

From Kona to Hawi, fifty-six desolate, deserted, hot, black, lava-covered miles lie in wait for the poor unsuspecting cyclists. And once out of the village for the third event, the by-now exhausted runners have to traverse that same desolation for the ten miles out past the airport to the marathon turnaround. There is nothing but deadly heat and boredom. The tedious mile after mile seems to just suck the energy, body fluids, and goals right out of the most committed of competitors.

These are the thoughts that were going through my mind all week long just before my sixth Ironman. I felt strong enough to continue hard training, but the word among all the triathletes is "taper." To taper means to ease off on all those hard miles of training so that the body can recover its energy and strength.

The most common mistake triathletes make is to go into a race tired. It is also very difficult to taper when you've got so much energy, you just **can't** sit still.

We all say we'll start our taper and then end up taking "just a short swim to loosen up the shoulders," or "just a short cycle to loosen up the legs," or "just a short run to get rid of some excess energy," and, of course, once started, it's like taking "just one potato chip." Can't be done!

THOU SHALT KNOW THE COURSE!

There were people swimming the evening before the race as well as those who arrived so late that they had no choice but to check out the course (swim, bike, and/or run) at practically the last minute. One of the cardinal rules of racing is "Know the course."

With the Kona Ironman, this is especially true, especially when there are competitors arriving from all over the world, many of whom have never even been to America, much less Kona, Hawaii.

This obviously presents quite a problem when the course covers over 140 miles, to say nothing of the frequently extreme conditions. One year the winds were so strong that they literally blew cyclists off their bikes. The ocean can be so rough that swimmers get too seasick to continue as their vomiting sucks the strength right out of their bodies. If you're a runner, you know what 114 degrees Fahrenheit can do to you. Needless to say, newly arrived competitors are anxious about the course.

One cannot even check out the course in the cool of the evening without grave risk since there aren't even any street lights. The dates of the Ironman are, in fact, selected on the basis of the lunar calendar, and the athletes have until midnight to finish. The light of a full moon is all there is to guide many of the competitors on their quest for the final finish line.

I had feelings of nervousness and anxiety constantly welling up in me. In spite of continuously reminding myself that I had done this several times before and could, therefore, do it again, I still felt very apprehensive. I almost envied those who were doing it for the first time; they, after all, did not yet **know how bad** it could get out there.

I also knew that, on each of the five previous Ironman events, that I had been on the better side of the odds, and that one of these days, those odds were going to catch up with me!

YOU'VE GOT MORE GUTS THAN I DO, LADY!

Some of the fears centered around mechanical problems with the bike. I ride racing wheels with 12 spokes in front and 18 on the rear. (The usual number of spokes is 36!) This concession to aerodynamics and weight does not inspire confidence in me or anyone who looks at these wheels, usually with great amazement! "Those wheels don't look like they could hold you up!" or "You've got more guts than I do, lady!" I have been assured, however, that they are as strong, if not stronger, than the conventionally 36-spoked wheel. And, so far, they've served me well. Five Ironman triathlons without a mishap or even getting out of true!

Oh, yes, there was an incident in one of the races when I THOUGHT I had a problem. I was coming down the home stretch of the bicycle leg, concentrating only on keeping up my speed.

All of a sudden there was a "tick, tick, tick" with each revolution of my front wheel. I was near panic! Expecting the wheel to collapse at any moment, I put on my brakes, trying to slow down so that when I fell, I wouldn't hit the pavement so hard.

Then I thought of stopping to try to fix the problem. All the insecurities I've ever had about my limited mechanical prowess came surging at me, and I took the cowardly way out. I kept pedaling!

The "tick, tick, tick" continued unabated but nothing else was happening. With my heart in my mouth, I decided to get as close to the bike finish line as possible so as to cut down the distance I would have to carry my bike to the bike transition point. (Triathlon rules say only that you and your bike have to finish; you don't have to be ON it! You can CARRY it!)

By this time my legs were rubbery and shaking as the panic-induced adrenalin was wearing off. I was, to say the least, a nervous wreck. But still, nothing was happening. The wheels were still turning with me still upright on the bike.

By this time the finish was in sight. I put on an extra surge of speed, crossed the finish line, dropped the bike, and took off running. It was only on completion of the run that I found out what had happened.

The sensor of my speedometer had loosened its attachment to the spoke and was dangling uselessly, hitting the brake with every revolution of the wheel. You can bet that I now frequently check for loose screws on the connector for that errant sensor!

Then there are all the things that can go wrong during the marathon leg. Every time I consider 26.2 miles alone, much less after a 2.4-mile swim and 112 miles of cycling, I still shake my head in disbelief. Logically, it seems to me that it can't be done, especially after some of my 100-mile training rides and the 112-mile Around Oahu Bike Race, when I can barely limp into the finish area.

But what this has taught me is that we do what we have to do, and if I program my mind, it will generally, I stress generally, keep the body going until the end—whenever it comes. This is how I cope with differing external and internal conditions.

What I see is what I get, and I just get on with it. It's not always foolproof as I am reminded periodically when I see one of the burned-out competitors staggering zombie-like in directions not always leading directly to the finish line.

A FALLEN ATHLETE

And what's even more heart-rending is to see a fallen athlete. It brings tears to my eyes as I wonder why and how our minds can push our bodies up to and even beyond their physiological limits.

What a demonstration of the power of the mind with its ability to set goals, to visualize their attainment, and the ability to perform what must be self hypnosis. I still marvel at the genus of this species! We're all pretty incredible when you stop to think about it!

THE SLEEP OF THE EXHAUSTED

One thing about heavy training that a lot of athletes notice: the anxiety may be pretty devastating but we can usually sleep very well. No matter how nervous I've been about these ultra-distance events, I've usually gotten a good night's sleep the night before. After all, I can hardly hold my eyes open past 9:00 p.m.. When I'm really nervous, I tend to wake up very early.

Since most races start at very early hours, it all works out very well. And with this much physical activity, one tends to sleep very soundly and seemingly to require less sleep. In fact, I feel that all the body's systems seem to work better with a heavy load of exercise and a good diet.

As it turns out, all those insecurities that come flooding up during the week preceding the Ironman serve a very useful purpose. One should never undertake an event like this lightly, no matter how many times you've done it.

Even if your conditioning was as good or better than in past events, there are always different conditions out there on the course. While it's true that the experience you've gained helps, no two events are ever identical. Nor are you ever exposed to all the risky situations that could ever come up.

LIFE IS NOT ALWAYS FAIR

Two weeks before the 1987 Kona Ironman, a competitor was hit by a concrete truck and killed. I knew Pat Griskus, having ridden alongside him in the 1986 Ironman when we were both trying to buoy each other's resolve to keep going at the 80-mile mark of the bike leg. Pat had lost a leg in a motorcycle accident some years prior. He had gotten an artificial leg, put running shoes on, and was out here doing the Ironman. Surely, I thought, if Pat can make it, so must I! How tragic that he did not make it, after all he'd been through!

Riding out in the middle of the lava fields at temperatures over 100 F., I was experiencing a terrible low. I wanted to get off that bike in the worst way and go stretch out on the lava. Reminding myself that the rough lava was no place to lie down, I negotiated with myself to try to keep going until I reached the next aid station.

Then, I reasoned, I could lie down where they have medical aid if I needed it. But the lava kept enticing me. It was not soft, fluffy, cushy, chocolate marshmallow — it's hard, hot, black molten rock! My God, I thought, I must be hallucinating.

Checking the speedometer, I calculated that the next aid station was only a couple of miles away. Surely, I could make it to that point, and THEN I could lie down. Then I started wondering why I was going through this. It had never happened before. Maybe people were right — three and four Ironman Triathlons in a year are too much for any body's body. Then I recalled that I had not eaten very much food, concentrating instead on fluids.

When I finally made it to the next aid station, I gobbled up everything in sight: bananas, oranges, cookies, and I can't remember what else. Within a few minutes, I could feel the energy coursing through my body. I now felt as if I could make it to the next aid station before lying down. I thought then that I would be able to at least finish the bike before lying down.

Then, when I finally got to the end of the bike, I thought I could at least run a couple of miles to make it a "complete" training day, and **THEN** I'd lie down.

EVEN A BED OF HOT LAVA CAN LOOK GOOD

After, a few miles I realized that I was feeling strong enough to run the entire marathon. I could not believe how I'd gone from the extreme of wanting so badly to lie down on that bed of hot lava to completing a marathon and crossing the finish line, feeling so fantastic that I babbled euphorically for three hours after!

That was the memory I had of Pat. He and I shared our feelings about questioning our sanity at even being out there, doing these painful things to our bodies. The shock hit hard as I stared in disbelief at the newspaper article announcing his death. Then I realized that this was not the first time this has happened, and that it could happen to any one of us at any time!

Are we crazy to put ourselves at such high exposure to risk? Are we playing Russian roulette with our lives? Well, what are the odds? If 1500 people are competitors and one gets killed, is this a reason to back out of the competition? Is not daily living a risk of one degree or another? Where do we put ourselves on the "risk continuum?"

I suppose the least amount of risk exposure is in our own bedroom (certainly not the kitchen or the bathroom). Does it make any sense to say, then, that we should spend our whole lives in our bedroom? Obviously not.

Then there's the other extreme. And I guess that's where the answer lies. We each have to determine how much risk we are willing to take in our lives. Without risk there can be no gain; we have to put ourselves on the starting line first.

Then there's the fact of life that people are more frequently sorry for what they did **NOT** do than anything they ever did. So, while I'm not saying everybody should get out there and ride bicycles on the highway or do an Ironman, I **am** saying that whenever I've taken a risk, I've usually been glad that I did.

Having been diagnosed as a breast cancer patient has made me even more of a risk-taker. For one thing I've often felt that I had nothing to lose; I was going to die anyway. And, of course, that's true. We will **ALL** die anyway.

The only thing that's in question is when and how. It's just that in my case, I know the probable "how" but not the "when." So my approach changed with the diagnosis of cancer. It made me a lot more gutsy! If I'm going to go, I'm going to have done something first.

EIGHT YEARS OUT!

Coming up now on eight years since the diagnosis, my mind conjured up two very contrasting images. One, projecting ahead 30 years with never a recurrence and feeling sad that I'd wasted all that time worrying, all those doctor's visits, tests, the specter of cancer shadowing everything I did.

Then my mind went to the immediate future. Maybe tomorrow would be the day the hospital would call to say that the tests showed that the cancer has spread in my body, that it was time to start some chemotherapy or radiation, or whatever. I would feel the despair of losing those good feelings of invulnerability that had slowly been re-forming in my mind as I got further away from the deadly diagnosis day.

So which was it to be? This says a lot for living in the present moment, doesn't it? Make each day count because that really is all any of us has.

A lot of these thoughts come up when I'm doing a long race. There are times when the present moment is extremely uncomfortable, and I wonder why I'm putting myself through this. These are the questions people ask when they are in any stage of life where there is discomfort.

The Ironman is a symbolic representation of life, a microcosm of a lifetime. There are the highs and lows in between the start and finish of an event, but there's nothing like getting the reward at the end. This is different for each one of us.

For me each time I have crossed that finish line, I have felt such joy and ecstasy that immediately cancels all the discomfort I'd felt just moments before.

Then I get to go around and see those who came in before me, sharing their joy. Next, I get to see those coming in after me and share their moments of finishing an incredible race.

The value of doing something like an Ironman or any of my other races usually is emphasized to me when I realize that my usual response after a short recovery period is "Just wait 'til next time!" And every "next time" has just gotten better and better! Wish it didn't have to end ever!

Fig. 20.1. Crossing the finish line, I felt such ecstasy and joy. Kona Photo Arts

CHAPTER TWENTY-ONE

WHAT'S THE PROGNOSIS:

WHY CANCER ISN'T CURABLE

Cancer is a very scary disease. Even with the advent of AIDS, it is considered the disease people fear the most. "Cancer patient" usually conjures up an image of a person ravaged by chemotherapy and radiation and then dying anyway!

Newspapers and magazines regularly report "breakthroughs" in cancer treatments, but the sad fact is that the most common cancers — colon, lung, breast, and prostate — have not been showing longer survival times. For one thing, by the time the cancer is detectable by the usual clinical methods, cancer cells have been shed by the tumor and spread throughout the body.

Once these cells break off from the primary tumor and are transported to other parts of the body through the circulatory system, it's almost impossible to detect the new colonies until they, too, are large enough to be picked up by blood tests, X-rays, scans, etc.

For chemotherapy and radiation to kill all of the cancer cells, the doses have to be so high they nearly kill the patient. These treatments can do irreversible damage to the patient's immune system, and this, after all, is what is keeping us alive. Without it, we are prey to every little bug that comes along.

HOW CANCER SPREADS

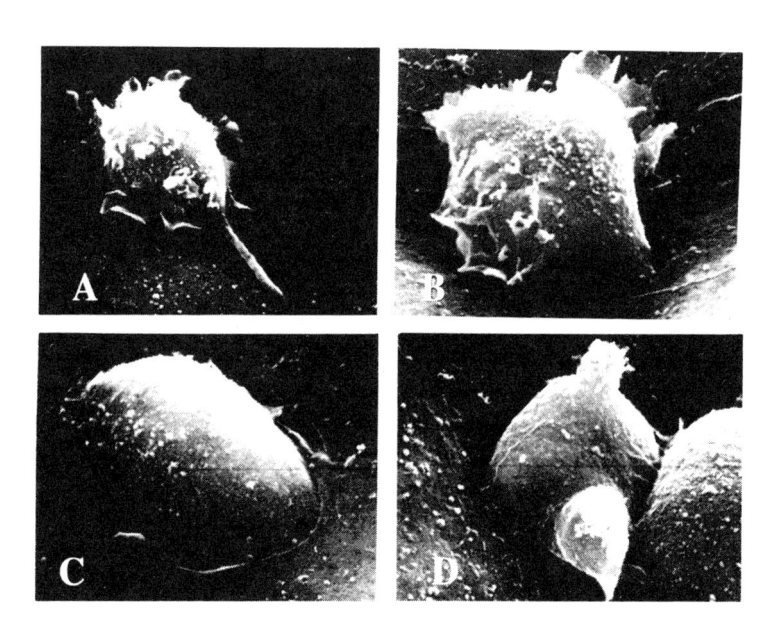

Fig. 21.1 (A) A metastatic cancer cell develops a pseudopod (false foot). (B) The pseudopod inserts itself into the wall of a blood vessel. (C) The metastatic cell enlarges the hole, penetrating the layers of the blood vessel. (D) The cancer cell then comes out the other side, hitching a ride via the blood stream to the lungs, liver, bones, and brain where it can set up a new colony of tumor cells (Based on electron microscopy images by Dr. Volker Schirrmacher).

Another important factor to consider is that with the improved diagnostic methods, the patient just finds out about his disease sooner. This artificially lengthens the "survival" time. The natural course of the disease in most cases is still the same, unfortunately.

HOW CANCER KILLS

What's confusing to a lot of people is how cancer kills. Right after my diagnosis, a few people said, "Well, it's just a breast." It's not usually the primary, or first, tumor discovered that is fatal, especially in breast, colon, prostate, and skin cancers. It's the metastasis, or spread, of these cells that break off and set up housekeeping in the liver, bones, lungs, and brain.

It's a lot like letting all the horses out of the barn. Tracking them down is extremely difficult, and shooting them down with chemicals and radiation is not only difficult, but it's also extremely hazardous to normal cells. That's why it causes nausea, vomiting, and hair loss.

The normal cells most vulnerable to these weapons are the fastest growing cells, the lining of our gastrointestinal system and hair. And if it's not powerful enough to cause those side effects, it's not likely to stop the cancer cells, either.

Because oncologists, or cancer specialists, are seeing so little change in the longevity of these patients with the most common kinds of cancer, many are starting to emphasize prevention. Through epidemiological (population) studies, it is very clear that individual countries have their own patterns of frequency of the different kinds of cancers. When many of these frequencies are correlated with dietary differences, a telling pattern emerges.

This is why so many researchers are convinced that colon, breast, and prostate cancers are related to diet. There are almost perfect correlations between frequency of deaths from breast cancer and percentage of dietary fat, according to the findings of K. Carroll, a researcher who published his findings in 1975.

A study was published by A. Lowenfels in 1977 showing that breast and colon cancer rise together in 56 countries of the world.

When you look at the similarity in the rising and falling of the cancer rates and the dietary fat, it is striking that all of the variance is explained. In other words, there isn't "room" left for other variables such as genetics, environment, stress, etc.

NATURE'S EXPERIMENT

So, while we cannot do the live-human experiments we would need to "prove" this theory, we can take advantage of this natural experiment provided us if we are smart enough to look at the data before us. The few countries who have a greater fat intake than we in the U.S., Netherlands, Denmark, New Zealand, for example, also have a greater death rate from breast cancer.

As early as 1963, Ernst Wynder, M.D. and President and founder of the American Health Foundation, noted the fact that Japanese women in Japan with breast cancer survived much longer than American breast cancer patients, even those of **Japanese** ancestry. These same findings are noted with animal studies, so this rules out genetics as the longevity factor.

There are other cancer types with dismal survival rates. Lung cancer, for example, has a five-year survival rate of less than 10 percent, meaning that fewer than 1 out of 10 are alive 5 years after their diagnosis. The Surgeon General's Report in 1979 reported that little significant progress in the diagnosis or treatment of lung cancer has been made in the last 15 years.

All that has changed since then is that the mortality rate of lung cancer in women surpassed that of breast cancer in 1987, clearly reflecting the increased smoking among females.

OH, FOR A MAGIC WAND!

If we could rule out two of the most preventable causes of cancers, i.e., smoking and high-fat diets, we would eliminate **most** of the cancers in this country and the whole

Western world. The ones remaining, the relatively rare types of cancer, are the ones that are yielding to the new advances in cancer therapies. This is such an exciting thought that I wish I had a magic wand and could just wave cigarettes and high-fat foods out of people's lives.

Given that this is an impossibility, there is an alternative that works. And that is to make **athletes** out of all smokers and fat-eaters! Once a person starts an athletic training program and then starts competing in races, which reinforces the training program, that person usually will not do those things which are counterproductive to winning.

This means that the person wins, the body wins, society wins, and nobody loses! There is no greater "high" than that of doing well in a race. And "well" doesn't necessarily mean placing first. For beginners, doing well means just finishing the race. For the more advanced, it means a PR, personal record, doing it faster than you've ever done it before. I've seen people jump up and down, scream, and generally just go crazy when they've set a new PR. It's THAT exciting for them.

Then there's the joy of "first place." That excitement or pride can last for years, plus it's usually made more tangible by a neat trophy or plaque. Now this is not to say that success comes easy. There **is** discomfort; there's sometimes pain! There were times during the Ironman that I felt extreme pain; the pain was intense enough that I wondered why I was putting myself through the agony.

But what I learned from earlier events was that the pain all of a sudden gets washed away with the euphoric joy of crossing that finish line. I never knew that it was anything but a feeling until I saw my first Ironman finish-line photograph. I was astounded at the expression on my face. I had never seen me look so ecstatic. And it's been repeated with every finish-line photo. There's just no substitute for the "high" that this kind of success can give.

Scientists have postulated it's the endorphins (chemicals the body makes that are similar to opiates) that make us feel so good at times like that.

Whether it's the endorphins or the purely intellectual joy of accomplishing a major goal is irrelevant. What IS relevant is that psychologically, there is a lot going on here, and it has to do with **survival**.

WHY SOME MAKE IT AND SOME DON'T

One of the great mysteries of cancer (and other diseases as well) has to do with why some people survive when they are not expected to and some die who were expected to survive. Remember, in my case the doctors at first could not tell me whether I had 3 months, 3 years, or how long.

A theory promoted by the Simontons in their book, *Getting Well Again*, deals with this very subject. Dr. Bernie Siegel in his book, *Love, Medicine, and Miracles* is onto the same thing. It seems to boil down to whether or not the patient has the will to fight the disease.

This will seems to be bolstered by visualization of the body's immune system actively engaging cancer cells in combat. As I was training over the hundreds of hours with my rhythmical pedaling, padding, or paddling, I was probably in a state of self-hypnosis. I was giving myself suggestions about how I was getting stronger, healthier, and having my white blood cells kill cancer cells.

Visualization is a relatively passive process. You're supposed to sit or lie quietly and picture strong, powerful white blood cells searching and destroying confused, weak cancer cells. While working on it, I found myself gritting my teeth, trying to make the visualization more "real." I tried, through closed eyes, to "see" those white blood cells gobbling up vagrant cancer cells. All I really saw was a velvety purple with flashes here and there, as my squinting caused pressure on my optic nerve.

It was a different matter on the playing field, however. This was an **active** process. Ha! What an understatement to call doing an Ironman "active." This was an entire day and part of a night spent swimming, biking, and running at race pace, feeling totally exhilarated, healthy, and in total control of my universe.

Those feelings for me are very real. No visualization is required. I'm on the move, attacking, in complete control of my life, and as far from passive as one can get.

As the feelings of fatigue start to creep up on me, I'm still battling on, except that now the "enemy" is real. My body is obeying all the commands to race for time in the senses of winning the race and winning in life. My body is functioning at its best while eating and drinking (that's part of the fun, too; I burn up around 10,000 calories doing an Ironman). I'm experiencing the full range of emotions, a microcosm of a lifetime, and gain a perspective of who I am and what I want. That, I suppose, could be called "active visualization" since I feel my healthiest while competing.

TAKING CONTROL

All this has to be good for the immune system in the long run. In the short run intense physical activity depresses the white blood cell count. For me, doing the Ironman was my way of taking control of my disease. Instead of doing nothing, or grasping at chemotherapy or radiation, I was being as active as I could possibly be.

It's only a hypothesis at this point but I feel that the feelings of loss of control when you are given the diagnosis of cancer is one of the deadliest things about this disease. And the only way I could counter that feeling and wrest control again was by setting my goal of doing an Ironman.

It's been said that about 20 percent of people who are seriously ill would prefer to die if given the opportunity. About 60 percent are willing to live providing the doctor does the work and the treatment is not too uncomfortable.

The final 20 percent say "I'll do **anything** to get well. Just tell me what I have to do!"

This book and the program herein is written for people in that last category. It is also written for those who have not yet been diagnosed with a serious illness but, if they had been, would fall in that last category. People who follow this type of program will successfully avoid the two major **preventable** killers of Americans, heart disease and cancer. I hope you are in this group.

The discoveries I have made along this multi-year journey to the Ironman have been exciting and revolutionary. At first, the medical community was totally against the ideas that diet, exercise, and anything mental could possibly make a difference in the survival of a cancer patient. Little by little I was feeling my way.

As I increased the exercise, I found my ability to take control was increasing. This also served as my psychological support. At the same time I started to see glimmerings in the press about the role of diet and exercise in the treatment of cancer patients.

About a year into this program I got a letter from two Ohio State University researchers with a request to fill out a questionnaire. They were onto the same thing I was.

Another year went by and I got a phone call from New York City (remember, I'm in Hawaii) from a national running magazine reporter who'd heard about my unusual approach to dealing with cancer. That interview culminated in a very nice story on me which led to a stories in *Newsday, USA Today, The Honolulu Star Bulletin,* and such international publications as the *New Zealand Herald,* the *Asahi Shimbun,* an Australian running magazine, the *Fun Runner,* and newspaper blurbs in Russia, Thailand, and Nepal.

More recently, there have been even more positive results in the studies that have been carried out. "Nine different, recently published studies have suggested that regular exercise might reduce the risk of cancer," says Randy Eichner, M.D., a hematologist at the University of Oklahoma Health Science Center in Oklahoma City.

These studies show that non-active women had about twice the risk of breast cancer and almost three times the rate of cancer of the ovaries, uterus, cervix, and vagina.

Additionally, active women had about half the rate of lymphoma, leukemia, myeloma, Hodgkin's disease, and cancer of the thyroid. There were also much lower rates in the incidence of other, less frequent types of cancer.

While these studies are on the "before" side of the equation, it is clear to me that whatever prevents cancer logically will have a role in the control and spread of cancer once it's established in the body. Some oncologists believe that whatever **initiates** cancer also **promotes** cancer!

So, does my approach work? A study by C. Barber Mueller, M.D., showed that 88 percent of the women who died following a diagnosis of cancer of the breast ultimately died of their breast cancer. This was a study utilizing data collected for 19 years by the Syracuse, N.Y. Upstate Medical Center Cancer Registry on 3,558 women. Since cancer cells can remain viable in vitro (in the laboratory) for up to **fifty** years, it's too soon to tell if my approach is working. Besides, an experiment of one is totally inadequate. What it can do, though, is point the way for others to try.

We need some controlled studies to see if cancer cells are really anaerobic as Ronald Lawrence, M.D., President of the American Medical Jogging Association, said.

GET "SUPER-FIT"

In the case of other patients who **REALLY** want to live, get yourself as fit as you can possibly be, or what I call "super-fit." Use the three-pronged approach of diet, exercise, and active visualization or self-hypnosis, and give it all you've got!

It's a *race* worth winning!

THE IRONMAN: A LIFETIME IN A DAY

I lived a lifetime in 13:33:18 hours on October 18, 1986. In that span of time there seemed to be a microcosm of life with an incredible range of emotions, sensations, and experiences.

—The wonderment I felt as I stood waiting for the starting gun, observing a thousand other bodies, all incredibly fit, strong, sensuous, and beautiful, and all would be put through paces that could cause real damage at their cellular level—the electrolytes that would unbalance, the stomachs that would refuse nourishment, the kidneys that would shut down, and eyes that would focus on nothing but that **FINISH LINE!**

—The physical battles I encountered in the swim as I held at bay and fended off hundreds of flailing arms. Even so, several found their mark and inflicted what I told myself was unintentional, anonymous pain—keep going, damn it...

—The mental battle during the bike leg as I wondered at the intelligence of one who gave up the "tried and true" (but slower) for the "state of the art", hi-tech (but of questionable reliability) and the "fun" of worrying for six and a half hours if I was going to have an equipment malfunction!

—The "**THIS IS IT!**" feeling I felt as I turned my body over to a set of conditioned responses—OK, legs, keep that pedal cadence at 100 rpm for the next 112 miles; the heat and your fatigue are to be totally irrelevant to the task at hand...

—The "**PEAK EXPERIENCE**" feeling I had as I was challenged by a competitor and the legs responded with a surge of power, almost as if I had nothing to do with it...

—My real battle with pain as my not-quite-healed stress fracture threatened blackmail: "If you don't stop, I'll fracture on you again," My mental reply: "If you don't keep going, I'll..." The implied threats worked!

—The surges of excitement I felt as I heard "**Go, Ruth, Go!**" from the sidelines, glancing briefly to see who was there; the surge of gratitude I felt when the face wasn't familiar but, held in their hands, was a race program from which they had obviously looked up to see who #523 was.

—The disappointment I felt as my finish time goals got adjusted from 11 hours, to 12 hours to 13 hours; and from setting a new age group record, to an age group first place, to just "get the damn thing over with"— **survival!**

—The joy I felt calculating that I had taken 45 minutes off last year's time, still placing to earn a "piece of hardware"—a beautiful plaque and an "Ironman" watch!

What a lifetime! And, just wait 'til next year!

APPENDIX I

INTERPRETATION OF LABORATORY TESTS

The following information is provided as a quick reference so that you can look up the results of your lab tests. Since there are variations between laboratories, this information is not guaranteed to be accurate. Use this as a rough guide to learn more about lab tests and what information they provide about your body.

CHOL (100-160 mg/dl): stands for blood cholesterol. This is probably the most important of all the blood tests. If you are average (220 mg/dl) then you have an average risk for heart attack (better than 50%), breast cancer (1 in 9 for women), colon cancer (1 in 20) and gallbladder disease (1 in 5). Cholesterol is found only in animal products, and conversely, all animal products contain cholesterol. Our own bodies make all the cholesterol we need. When we eat additional cholesterol in the form of animal products, it is readily absorbed. The problem develops because our livers can only break down a limited amount of this substance per day. The excess accumulates in body tissues like arteries, skin, organs, and body fat. Your blood level reflects the level of cholesterol in your body. The ideal level is 160 mg/dl or less. Replacing animal foods with starches, vegetables, and fruits will cause the cholesterol to fall 30-100 mg/dl in most people in less than 21 days. Maintenance of this diet will result in continued improvement. Excreted cholesterol enters the gallbladder, thereby contributing to gallstones (90% are made of cholesterol). Cholesterol in the colon is believed to be involved in colon cancer. Eating vegetable oils will cause more cholesterol to be excreted with a rise in a person's risk of gallbladder disease and colon cancer. A change to a no-cholesterol diet is the most effective and safest way to lower your cholesterol. All plant foods contain NO cholesterol. Coconuts and chocolate contain enough saturated fat to raise cholesterol levels in the blood.

HDL (Male 26-66 mg/dl; Female 30-75 mg/dl): stands for High Density Lipoprotein, a fraction of the total cholesterol with some predictive value for risk of heart disease. HDL is an end product of cholesterol metabolism and represents the cholesterol that is leaving the tissues on the way to being excreted by the liver. If your level is low and you're consuming the typical American diet, you should consider this an indication that it's time to start a low/no cholesterol diet. People on low cholesterol diets have low HDL because of the low total cholesterol.

GLUCOSE (65-120 mg/dl): the sugar in your blood. When you haven't eaten for awhile, the level is normally between 65 and 120 mg/dl. The body can lose control of sugar levels, the condition called diabetes (levels over 120 mg/dl.) Most diabetes (95%) is the so-called adult-onset Type II, and is caused by a high fat, low-fiber diet. Correction of the diet will solve this problem for most people. Exercise and weight loss also help. Type I, childhood-onset diabetes, is a different condition that results from destruction of portions of the pancreas that produce insulin. While diet will not cure this type, a proper diet will certainly help. Hypoglycemia is a condition of low blood sugar (below 50 mg/dl). Another test (the 5-hour glucose tolerance test) is used to make this diagnosis. The cause and correction are diet.

BUN (6-25 mg/dl): stands for Blood Urea Nitrogen, the breakdown products of protein. BUN is made in the liver and excreted by the kidneys. Low protein diets lower BUN. Kidney disease can cause the BUN to rise and make people feel ill.

CREA (0.7 - 1.4 mg/dl): stands for creatinine, a breakdown product from muscle, excreted by the kidneys. Elevation usually means kidney disease.

URIC ACID (2.2-7.7 mg/dl): a breakdown product of purines which are found in high protein foods such as meat, seafood, chicken, cheese, and beans. Large amounts of uric acid can lead to gout (arthritis) and kidney stones.

TRIG (50-275 mg/dl): stands for triglycerides, blood fats. If your blood were to stand in a test tube overnight, a layer of fat would rise to the top. High levels are associated with heart attacks, diabetes, and poor circulation which result in chest pain, leg pain, and fatigue. Triglycerides are elevated by consuming alcoholic beverages, simple sugars and fats. Even fruit and fruit juice can elevate the levels in sensitive people. Exercise, high fiber foods and weight loss will lower triglycerides to healthy levels. Note that sometimes during a period of weight loss, triglycerides may temporarily rise due to the movement of

CL (96-110 meq/l) and **CO2** (25-32 meq/l): stands for chlorine and carbon dioxide, usually at normal levels in the blood unless people are on medications.

TOT PRO (6.2-8.3 g/dl): stands for total protein which represents the protein floating in the blood. These proteins are made primarily by the liver and the immune system. They may be elevated in certain infections and disease of the bone marrow.

ALBUMIN (3.6-5.2 g/dl): a protein made in the liver, down in serious liver and kidney disease.

GLOBULIN (2.5 g/dl): the protein made by the immune system for defense.

A/G (1.1-2.2): stands for the ratio of albumin to globulin.

HEMOGLOBIN (Male 14-18 gm/dl; Female 12-16 gm/dl): the oxygen-carrying, red-pigmented, iron-containing substance in the blood. The level reflects the amount of red blood cells in the body, and a low level can mean anemia. Twenty percent of women in this country have iron deficiency anemia. Dairy products contribute to this problem in several ways. Cow's milk is deficient in iron, and the calcium and phosphorus in cow's milk complexes iron from other sources to prevent absorption. The fats in dairy products and other foods cause higher levels of estrogen in a woman's body with resulting heavier menstrual periods with more blood loss each month. Anyone with anemia should be checked for blood loss in their stools, at the minimum.

HCT (40-55%, slightly lower in women): Hematocrit shows the percentage of blood cells (mostly red blood cells) comprising the total blood volume. Used as a test for anemia and dehydration, and to follow the course of therapy for anemia.

TIBC (200-400 mcg/100 ml): stands for Total Iron-binding Capacity and is usually increased only with an iron deficiency anemia, a type of anemia usually associated with blood loss.

SERUM FERRITIN (30 ng/100ml and up): a measure of the iron stores in the body. Decreased ferritin is found with iron deficiency but not with an anemia of infection. Increased ferritin is found with excessive iron intake.

fat from the fat tissues to the blood. You should try to keep your levels below 200 mg/dl.

BILI (1l0-1.7 mg/dl): a breakdown product of red blood cells. It is elevated when there is a large breakdown of blood cells, and when the liver is diseased and unable to adequately excrete it. Many people have a slight elevation (up to 3 mg/dl) that may occur as a result of overnight fasting. The best indication of normal is that all the other liver tests are normal.

SGOT (7-50 U/L), **SGPT** (7-50 U/L), **LDH** (90-225 U/L): abbreviations for liver enzymes that are released when the liver is injured. Gallbladder disease, excess alcohol consumption and viruses causing hepatitis are the most common causes of elevation.

ALK PHOS (30-115 U/L): stands for alkaline phosphatase, an enzyme from either the bones or the liver. It can be elevated in bone or gallbladder disease.

INORG P (2.0-4.7 mg/dl): stands for inorganic phosphorus. Levels increase with amount of phosphorus in your diet.

CALCIUM (8.8-10.8 MG/DL): a mineral with many functions in the body. Blood levels must be kept at minimum critical levels. Therefore, calcium levels are almost always normal. Abnormal values usually reflect laboratory error or a decrease in the albumin protein in the blood, due to liver or kidney disease. The level of calcium in your blood does not reflect the amount of calcium in your diet or in your bones.

NA (135-145 meq/l): stands for sodium, a mineral found in large quantities in the body. The level does not reflect your dietary intake of salt. Sometimes the level is low when people are taking diuretics, medications to lower blood pressure.

K (3.5-5.5 meq/l): stands for potassium, a mineral also found in large amounts in the body. Levels do not reflect dietary intake unless you have serious kidney disease. Sometimes the level is low when people are on diuretics. This mineral must be kept in the normal range or death can result.

APPENDIX TWO

GLOSSARY

Aerobic Integrity: A level of oxygen-burning exercise where the body can maintain a sustained output for an extended period of time without going into oxygen debt.

Amnesia: Lack or loss of memory. **Anterograde a.**, loss of memory for events which occurred since the onset of the disease. **retrograde a.**, loss of memory for events which occurred before the onset of the disease.

Anaerobic: An inability to maintain an oxygen level in the body to support con-tinued exercise. Leads to oxygen debt.

Anemia: Deficient quantity or quality of the blood. Usually marked by paleness and fatigue.

Areola: The pigmented area surrounding the nipple.

Biathlon: Any two-sport race, for example, a swim-run, or a bike-run.

Biceps: The muscle of the upper arm.

Biopsy: Examination of tissue removed from a living subject.

Carbohydrate: Starchy and sugary foods; compounds made up of carbon in groups of six atoms, and hydrogen and oxygen in proportions to form water. Has 4 calories/gm.

Chemotherapy: Treatment by powerful chemical compounds which have a toxic effect on specific cells or micro-organisms. Cancer cells, which are frequently weak and disorganized, are usually more vulnerable to the effects of the drugs.

Cholesterol: A waxy substance produced in the liver of all animals. Makes up the structural integrity of all animal cells.

Endorphins: Chemicals produced by the body which produce pleasant feelings. Contributes to the so-called "runner's high."

Epidemiology: The branch of science that deals with the occurrence, distribution and types of diseases; population studies.

Fascia: the band or sheet of connective tissue covering the muscles.

Fat: The oily substance that covers the connective tissues of animals; an organic salt consisting of the glycerol radical, C_3H_5, combined with a fatty acid. Has more than twice the number of calories of carbohydrate and protein, 9 calories/gm.

Hydrostatic body fat test: A method of estimating percent of body fat by immersion in water.

Infiltrating ductile carcinoma: Moderately metastasizing, invasive breast cancer accounting for about 65 percent of all breast cancers. May spread to liver, lungs, bones, and brain. Usually cannot be eradicated by local treatment of breast and lymph nodes. Usually has spread to bloodstream by the time clinical symptoms are evident.

Lacto-ova-vegetarian: A person who avoids all animal products except dairy products and eggs. This diet will still be high in animal fat and cholesterol. Milk has been referred to as "liquid meat."

Liposuction: A surgical procedure whereby fat is sucked out of the body in very specific areas.

Marathon: A footrace of 26.2 miles. Originated in Greece in 490 B.C. When the Athenians defeated the Persians, a messenger, Phidipides, was sent to bear the news of the victory to Athens. The name is derived from his run starting at Marathon. Now, most cities and countries of the world conduct these races annually.

Mastectomy: The surgical amputation of the breast; **modified radical m.** removal of breast plus skin, nipple, subcutaneous fat, fascia, and axillary (armpit) nodes; **simple m.** removal of breast tissue only, leaving skin and nipple; **radical m.** removal of breast, skin, nipple, fascia, subcutaneous fat, axillary nodes, and the pectoral (chest) muscles; **lumpectomy**: removal of the tumor and a margin of healthy tissue surrounding tumor.

Metastasis: Spread of disease from one organ to another. Cancerous cells break off from the primary tumor and invade the bloodstream or lymphatics. Once there, these cells travel to other parts of the body, such as the lungs, liver, bones, and brain, setting up new cancerous tumor colonies.

Okole: Hawaiian word for "buttocks."

Oncology, -ist: The study of tumors and cancers.

Opu nui: Hawaiian for "large stomach."

Osteoporosis: The thinning of the bones, abnormal porousness, the cause of which is still debated. Most recent studies show that the best treatment, as well as prevention, is exercise and a low protein diet.

Protein: Combinations of amino acids and their derivatives found in animal and vegetable tissues. Has 4 calories/gm.

Reconstructive breast surgery: The insertion of an implant under the skin to restore the normal body contours when lost due to an amputated breast. Nipples and areolae may also be reconstructed by using various body parts such as ear lobes, skin from the upper inner thigh, etc.

"Run To The Sun" Race: A footrace of 37 miles from sea level to the 10,000 ft.top of Haleakala, "House of the Sun" on Maui.

Subcutaneous: Under the skin. May refer to implant placement when used in recon- structive breast surgery as opposed to sub-muscular, under the chest muscle.

Triathlon: Any three-sport race; conventionally, a swim, bike, run.

Ultramarathon: Any footrace longer than a marathon (26.2 miles).

Vegan: A vegetarian diet that is devoid of all animal products, including dairy products and eggs. Biochemically, there is very little difference in the composition of meat, dairy products and eggs. All animal products are high in fat, high in cholesterol, and low in fiber and iron.

BIBLIOGRAPHY

The McDougall Plan, John A. McDougall, M.D., New Century Publishers, 1983.

The McDougall Program, John A. McDougall, M.D., NAL Books, 1990.

McDougall's Medicine, John A. McDougall, M.D., New Century Publishers, 1985.

Vegan Nutrition: Pure and Simple, Michael Klaper, M.D., Gentle World, 1997.

Aerobics, Kenneth Cooper, M.D., Bantam Books, 1968.

Fit Or Fat, Covert Bailey, Houghton Mifflin Co., 1978.

Getting Well Again, O. Carl Simonton, M.D., Stephanie Matthews-Simonton, J. P. Tarcher, Inc. 1978.

Love, Medicine & Miracles, Bernie Siegel, M.D., Harper & Row, 1986.

Superlearning, Sheila Ostrander, Lynn Schroeder, Dell Publishing, 1979.

Stand Tall! Morris Notelovitz, M.D., Marsha Ware, Triad Publishing, 1982.

How A Woman Ages, Robin Henig, Ballantine Books, 1985.

The Illustrated Swimmer, Jan Prins, Ph.D., Honolulu He'e, 1982.

Triathlon Training, Dave Scott, Simon & Schuster, 1986.

Bicycle Road Racing, Edward Borysewicz, Velo-News, 1985.

A Weight Control Workbook, Carl S. Weisbrod, HWA Publishers, 1990

Choices, Realistic Alternatives in Cancer Treatment, Marion Morra and Eve Potts, Avon Publishers, 1980.

Diet For A New America, John Robbins, Stillpoint Publishing, 1987.